SISKIYOU CC
LI
609
YRE

D0391716

## PAPERBACK PLUS

# Contents

67750

# About
# Rick Archbold

**Rick Archbold** has known Robert Ballard since he began working with him on the text of *The Discovery of the Titanic* in 1986.

Mr. Archbold says of Dr. Ballard, "Bob is always excited about the new projects he wants to undertake. In some ways he's an eternal kid, with the ability to bring a sense of wonder to every adventure."

Canadian writer and editor Rick Archbold has also collaborated with Dr. Ballard on *The Lost Wreck of the Isis, The Discovery of the Bismarck, Exploring the Bismarck,* and *The Lost Ships of Guadalcanal.*

He lives in Toronto, Canada.

# DEEP-SEA EXPLORER

The Story of Robert Ballard,
Discoverer of the *Titanic*
by Rick Archbold

HOUGHTON MIFFLIN COMPANY
BOSTON
ATLANTA   DALLAS   GENEVA, ILLINOIS   PALO ALTO   PRINCETON

**Acknowledgments**

For each of the selections listed below, grateful acknowledgment is made for permission to excerpt and/or reprint original or copyrighted materials, as follows:

**Selections**

*Deep Sea Explorer: The Story of Robert Ballard, Discoverer of the Titanic,* by Rick Archbold. Copyright © 1994 by The Madison Press Limited, published by Scholastic Inc. Reprinted by permission of The Madison Press Limited.

"Titanic: Destination Disaster," by John L. Lipp, from April 1992 *Plays* magazine. Copyright © 1992 by Plays, Inc. Reprinted by permission of *Plays, the Drama Magazine for Young People.*

"Titanic Diagram," from *Exploring the Titanic,* by Robert D. Ballard, illustrated by Ken Marschall. Copyright © 1988 by The Madison Press Limited, published by Scholastic Inc. Reprinted by permission of The Madison Press Limited.

**Illustrations**

**146–147, 152, 156–157, 162–163** John Gamache.

**Photography**

**145** The Bettmann Archive (tr). **149** Illustrated London News. **152** Ken Marschall Collection (r). **156** The Bettmann Archive (r). **157** The Bettmann Archive (l).

1997 Impression

Houghton Mifflin Edition, 1996

Copyright © 1996 by Houghton Mifflin Company. All rights reserved.

No part of this work may be reproduced or transmitted in any form or by any means, electronic or mechanical, including photocopying and recording, or by any information storage or retrieval system without the prior written permission of the copyright owner unless such copying is expressly permitted by federal copyright law. With the exception of nonprofit transcription in Braille, Houghton Mifflin is not authorized to grant permission for further uses of this work. Permission must be obtained from the individual copyright owner as identified herein. Address requests for permission to make copies of Houghton Mifflin material to School Permissions, Houghton Mifflin Company, 222 Berkeley Street, Boston, MA 02116.

Printed in the U.S.A.

ISBN: 0-395-73272-7

456789-B-99 98 97 96

# CONTENTS

To Jennifer,
whose voyage of discovery is just beginning.

# PROLOGUE

## July 13, 1986

FOR MORE THAN TWO HOURS, THE TINY SUBMARINE had been sinking through darkness blacker than any starless night. The enormous pressure of the water on *Alvin*'s metal hull was almost five hundred times that of the earth's atmosphere at sea level, more than enough to squeeze the air out of a human body. Three men were crammed into the six-foot wide sphere-shaped cabin: pilot Ralph Hollis, copilot Dudley Foster, and forty-four-year-old oceanographer Robert Ballard. But they weren't worried. *Alvin* had made countless visits to such depths before.

Ballard stretched as best he could in the cramped space, trying to restore circulation to his hip, which had gone to sleep during the descent. As he did so, his arm brushed the inside of the hull. The metal felt ice-cold and was wet from condensed moisture. He shivered, then stared again through the Plexiglas of the starboard viewport. Although the sub was rapidly approaching the bottom, two-and-a-half miles down, he could see nothing but blackness. Yet somewhere, only a few hundred yards away, lay the wreck of the *Titanic*.

"We're lost," Ralph Hollis reported, annoyance in his voice. "The surface navigator is driving us in circles."

Ballard muttered to himself in disgust. This was all he needed. An earlier problem with one of the sub's two batteries meant their time on the bottom would be brief. The batteries were *Alvin's* main source of power. If they failed before the sub resurfaced, only the back-up batteries stood between the three men and certain death. Now, with no means of navigating underwater, their chances of actually locating the wreck looked slim. It had taken Ballard thirteen long years to reach this point. But it seemed as though technical glitches would prevent him from setting eyes on the most famous shipwreck in history. He could hardly believe his bad luck.

The pings from the echo sounder, which told them how far they had yet to fall, indicated the ocean floor was now about six hundred feet below. But Hollis didn't slow down the sub. As a seasoned *Alvin* pilot, he waited until the last minute—only about a hundred feet from touchdown—to drop the descent weights. Suddenly lighter, the sub immediately slowed. And, with the outside lights now switched on, Ballard watched out his viewport as the bottom gradually materialized out of the dark-green gloom. There was no sign of wreckage, not a single piece of *Titanic* debris. All he could see outside the small, round window was a gently rolling plain of mud as a light "snow" of underwater particles fell past him. This was a view he'd seen many times before.

As *Alvin*'s single "ski" lightly touched bottom, the warning buzzer came on, indicating the battery problem was becoming critical. Only a few minutes remained before they would have to end the dive and head back to the surface. The *Titanic* was probably only a few hundred feet away, but in which direction was anybody's guess.

"Let's drive south," Ballard suggested, figuring that the deep-sea current had pushed them north of the wreck. Hollis cautiously piloted the sub along the bottom, its single ski leaving a lone track in the ooze. The alarm buzzer grew louder. Time was running out.

"*Alvin*, this is *A-II*." It was the surface navigator calling on the acoustic telephone from the mother ship, the *Atlantis II*, back at the surface. "Tracking is now working. The *Titanic* should bear fifty yards to the west of your present location." The system that allowed *Alvin* to know its precise position was once again functioning. And it revealed that Ballard's guess had been a good one. They had only barely missed the wreck.

Hollis promptly turned *Alvin* left, to the west. Suddenly the scene through Ballard's viewport changed dramatically. Instead of a smooth carpet of bottom sediment, he now stared at an unnaturally steep slope that looked as if it had been piled up by a gigantic underwater bulldozer. The alarm buzzer grew even louder and tension inside the sub mounted.

"Come right," Ballard almost shouted. He thought he'd seen something—a black wall coming out of the darkness.

Hollis turned the sub and inched it painstakingly forward, all the time peering intently through the forward viewport. Suddenly he brought *Alvin* to a full stop. Now each man in turn looked out the forward window. The sight that met their gaze was different from any they had encountered over hundreds of dives into the deep ocean. The nose of the sub was almost touching a seemingly endless slab of black metal rising out of the ocean floor. Ballard knew that he and his crew were the first human beings to see the hull of the R.M.S. *Titanic* in almost seventy-five years. In April 1912, on its maiden voyage, the supposedly unsinkable new passenger ship had hit an iceberg and sank, taking more than fifteen hundred of its twenty-two hundred passengers with it.

There was no time, however, to think about the significance of this moment of discovery. Hollis had already dropped *Alvin's* weights, lightening the submarine so that it began to accelerate toward the surface, soon reaching its maximum ascent speed of one hundred feet per minute. Would his first brief glimpse of the *Titanic* also be his last? Ballard wondered. He prayed that the battery problem would be fixable and that his dream of landing on the *Titanic's* deck would yet become a reality.

## CHAPTER 1

# SOMETHING HIDDEN

ROBERT BALLARD'S FIRST STRONG MEMORIES OF childhood come from Pacific Beach, California, a sleepy San Diego suburb to which his family moved in the summer of 1948. He was six years old.

Pacific Beach was a paradise for a small boy. Come spring, which in southern California means late March or early April, he'd kick off his shoes and pull off his shirt and hardly put them back on until November. With his older brother, Dick, or his best friend, Johnny Binkley, those bare feet trod every inch of San Diego Bay. The shore of the bay was an almost unspoiled wilderness of tidal pools and salt marshes full of marine life. The boys could spend hours by a tidal pool, observing the small fish, crabs, sea anemones, and starfish. They learned to swim in the warm, shallow water off the long, sandy beaches. Bob loved to dive underwater and hold his breath as long as possible. For some reason, he always preferred being under the water to floating on top of it.

Like many small boys who live close to nature, Bob often brought home specimens for closer examination. On one occasion, he came home from a seashore excursion and immediately locked himself in the bathroom. Eventually, his mother, Harriett Ballard, came to the door and opened the lock with a screwdriver. She found her son lying in a full bathtub with a huge frog floating on his stomach. "It needed a bath, Mom," he told her.

Bob was a happy-go-lucky child with boundless energy. Even though he was short for his age, this never held him back. He was always on the go. His mother still remembers a day when he was two years old. Twice he climbed over the high backyard fence and ended up at a local grocery store. The third time he tried this stunt she tied him to the clothesline with a jump rope. He got the message.

The Pacific shore was more than a playground for Bob Ballard. He was fascinated by the sea—its different moods, the movement of the tides, the strange animals that lived in it. He and Johnny Binkley liked to scare themselves with stories of the monsters that they imagined inhabited the ocean. The scariest creature actually living in San Diego Bay was the manta ray, popularly called the devil fish. It looks like a huge underwater bat with wings that can be as wide as twenty-two feet across. Actually it's quite harmless and has even been known to play games with scuba divers. But the boys preferred to believe that the manta ray was really an ocean devil and that it was out to get them.

For a look at other deep-sea creatures, they had only to visit the public aquarium at the Scripps Institution of Oceanography in La Jolla, then a small town about thirteen miles north of downtown San Diego. This was a favorite family outing. Bob could gaze forever at deadly looking sharks, creepy octopuses and squid, snakelike moray eels, and unbelievably colorful tropical species like the parrot fish.

In Ballard's memory, those San Diego years seem like one long, endless summer at the seaside. And young Bob seems like a modern version of Mark Twain's Tom Sawyer. However, like all true stories, it wasn't quite that simple.

Some time after Bob's baby sister, Nancy, was born, their mother began to worry that something was wrong. The infant was very slow to learn to walk. When it came time to talk, she didn't—not a single word. It gradually became clear that Nancy, who is four years younger than Bob, had a serious developmental problem. Nonetheless his parents were determined to give her as normal a life as possible. They searched endlessly for therapy that would help. Nothing worked. When teachers at school couldn't cope, the Ballards hired private tutors. Nancy learned to read and write, but speaking was impossible. Many years later they discovered that she had been born with a birth defect that harms the part of the brain governing speech.

Nancy's handicap affected Bob deeply. He loved his little sister and simply couldn't understand why she wouldn't talk to him. He became very upset and for a time had trouble in elementary school. But gradually everyone, including Nancy, learned to live with the situation. She became a passionate sports fan, keeping track of all the statistics of her favorite teams and always going to watch her brothers play. Not surprisingly, Bob and Dick were extremely protective of her.

In some ways, Nancy's problem brought the Ballards even closer together. Bob's parents placed a special emphasis on family activities that their daughter could share. They would often go camping in the mountains. And later, when the Ballards moved up to Los Angeles and bought a cabin cruiser, it was named the *Nancy Ann*. Nancy loved to fish, and the family spent many weekends fishing and snorkeling around Catalina Island, which lies just off the California coast near Los Angeles.

Bob Ballard now says that his sister's situation had a powerful impact on his own attitude to life. "Knowing Nancy would never be able to go out in the world and lead a 'normal' life made me twice as determined to make the most of my opportunities. I had this strong sense, even as a fairly young kid, that because I had been blessed with health and intelligence, it would have been sinful to squander these gifts. Nancy's handicap gave me a sense of urgency."

Even without Nancy's inspiration, Bob's drive to succeed would have been strongly nurtured by his parents, who fed him and his brother, Dick, strong and consistent messages about themselves. According to Dick, who is two years older than Bob, "My mother wrote the book on positive thinking." She repeatedly told her sons that they could be anything they wanted to be, in Dick's words that "they were destined for greatness." Both boys idolized their father, Chester Ballard. They especially loved speculating about his youth spent working on a ranch in Montana. In the family photograph album there was a photo of him, aged sixteen or so, standing with a rifle in his hand beside a bear he had shot. In the picture their father wore the broadest smile you could imagine. For Bob and Dick, this was proof positive that their dad, as they told their friends, had been a real cowboy.

In San Diego, Chester Ballard worked in the top-secret world of military hardware, helping to design ballistic missiles. The fact that he couldn't talk about his work added to his aura. So did the fact that he set very high standards for his sons. One of his favorite sayings was, "You've got to be so good that luck can't beat you." Once, in elementary school, when Dick came home with sterling grades, his father told him, "It's not enough to be smart, you've got to learn to be wise." Chester Ballard expected Bob and Dick to do well at everything they attempted, whether it was Boy Scouts, team sports, or deep-sea fishing. It was a difficult standard to live up to.

Bob remembers his father as a mostly distant figure, absorbed in his work. To be like him seemed an impossible goal. What's more, Dick was a star student, regularly bringing home a report card of straight A+'s. There was no way of bettering his older brother in academics. But, as a naturally gifted athlete, Bob could compete on the playing field. And, as a naturally gifted talker, he quickly learned how to hold the floor.

As Dick remembers it, the nightly game around the dinner table was to see who could get and hold their father's attention and make him laugh. Sometimes Bob and Dick were allies. But it was always Bob who would start the ball rolling by inventing some outrageous story. He was a born story-teller and clown, who had the ability to embellish and embroider a tale. His mother says now, "With Bob it was never one million. It was always one hundred and ten million."

Harriett Ballard would often take the children to spend the weekend at her parents' retirement home in Silverado Canyon in a beautiful part of the coastal mountains of southern California. For Bob these visits were magical. He would wake up early in the morning when the air was still chilly and snuggle under the warm quilt until his grandmother got up and started the wood stove. From after breakfast until it got dark he would roam the canyon, much of which was still wilderness. It was almost as fascinating as the ocean.

Bob's grandfather died when Bob was still a little boy and he has few memories of him. But everyone says Bob takes after him. Jack May loved people and he loved selling. He worked most of his life as a

(Above) The Ballard family, at Christmas Eve dinner, 1951. From front to left, Nancy, Chester, Dick, nine-year-old Bob, and Harriett. (Left) A younger Bob, at left, poses with his father and older brother, Dick. (Below) Bob, at seven, shows off his first fish.

salesman. According to his daughter, "He could sell you your own false teeth if you weren't careful." He was also wonderfully gregarious. He would go up to strangers and soon be on a first-name basis. Bob's mother is the same way. And so is Bob.

After his grandfather's death in 1950, when Bob was eight years old, his grandmother often came to stay with them. As a result he came to know her very well. She was the daughter of German immigrants who had settled in Kansas in the mid-nineteenth century. She had a warm heart and a very strict moral code. And she was quite easy to tease. Bob says now, "You could tell her the word *gullible* wasn't in the dictionary and she would believe you."

Although he enjoyed pulling her leg, Bob also listened to his grandmother's simple wisdom. Many of her favorite sayings stay with him to this day. One was: "When you enter a room, leave it better than you found it." Another one was: "Great is the person who plants a tree, knowing he will never sit in its shade."

In the summer of 1953, after five years in San Diego, the Ballards moved to Downey, California. Downey was a prosperous bedroom community that was developing on former farmland south of downtown Los Angeles. Like Bob's father, many of Downey's residents worked at North American Aviation's new missile division on the outskirts of town. Chester Ballard's new job was a step up the career ladder for him, but that wasn't the main reason for the move. He refused to believe the doctors who said that his daughter, Nancy, now seven years old, would never learn to talk. He'd heard about an experimental program in speech therapy being offered at the University of Southern California. He moved the family to Los Angeles so Nancy could enter the program.

The experimental therapy didn't work, but the family found Downey a wonderful place to live. The town was sprouting with housing subdivisions, but these bordered on undeveloped land—orchards and orange groves, many of them left untended and wonderful places for kids to play. The homes were spacious, rambling, single-story affairs, mostly covered in stucco and painted in pastel colors. Station wagons sat in the driveways beside neatly manicured lawns. More often than not, a swimming pool filled the backyard. Downey also boasted one of the first McDonald's in the world, only a short bicycle ride away from the comfortable three-bedroom house the Ballards moved into at 9314 Bigby Avenue. The only blot on the picture was the smog. In the early fifties, Los Angeles was rapidly becoming the freeway city it is today, in the process giving the world this new word to describe the fog caused by unfiltered automobile exhaust. Sometimes the smog got so thick you couldn't see to the end of the Ballards' block.

Now eleven, Bob was still short for his age. He didn't start to sprout up toward his current six feet until high school. But he had inborn athletic ability.

Downey was a sports-mad town and Bob fit right in. It seemed he could excel at any game he turned to. In high school he eventually became a star in basketball, football, and tennis. He became so good at tennis that he was soon taking lessons from the pro who taught Billie Jean King, later a Wimbledon champion. Sports was one area where his brother, Dick, could not compete with him.

Summers in Downey were the best, particularly after Bob got his first car, a fire-engine-red, two-door '54 Ford, and his first serious girlfriend, Diane Hinman, whom he started dating in his junior year. She wore his class ring on a chain around her neck and knitted a mirror warmer for his car. Most of Bob's friends spent their days at Huntingdon Beach Lifeguard Station Number 3, which was the exclusive turf of the Downey High School crowd. It was a scene out of a Beach Boys song—sunbathing, surfing, volleyball, and girls.

Bob became a skilled body surfer—he still preferred being in the water to being on top of it. He also learned to scuba dive. Soon it became one of his major pastimes. During long, warm, summer evenings he and his friends would hang out at McDonald's, sitting on their cars, shooting the breeze and drinking endless Cokes. (He loves Coke to this day.) Rock 'n' roll music and surfer dances like the Surfer Stomp and the Bear Hug were the rage.

Despite Bob's success with girls and sports, he says now that he always felt somehow apart. Outwardly he was preoccupied with the same things his friends were: cars, sports, taking his girlfriend on a date to Hollywood. But he kept his inner life to himself. His early fascination with what was hidden under the ocean had grown into a fascination with explorers of all kinds, but above all, ocean explorers.

Bob was mesmerized by the idea of submarine travel. Inspired by Jules Verne's famous fantasy novel, *Twenty Thousand Leagues Under the Sea*, he dreamed of exploring the world beneath the oceans. The novel's main character was the mysterious outlaw Captain Nemo, who circled the globe and visited a host of underwater wonders in his electricity-powered submarine, the *Nautilus*. Bob fantasized about standing at the controls of the *Nautilus*, battling the giant squid, fighting free from the grip of an Antarctic ice floe, or exploring the submerged ruins of the lost city of Atlantis. But he was also attracted to Captain Nemo himself, this strange, brooding loner whose past was never revealed, who made his own rules and lived by them.

As his junior year at high school drew to a close, while most of his friends were thinking about jobs as lifeguards or at McDonald's or as counselors at a summer camp, Bob was thinking about the Scripps Institution of Oceanography in San Diego. He hadn't forgotten the Scripps aquarium where he had spent those spellbound hours as a kid. In the spring of 1959, he entered a contest sponsored by the National Science Foundation for high school students interested in oceanography. The winners would become summer trainees at Scripps. Bob decided to enter the competition and labored over his brief essay on why he was interested in the ocean.

A few weeks after he sent it in, he received the answer. He had been chosen!

In early June, only a couple of weeks before his seventeenth birthday, Bob's parents drove him down the coast to San Diego. Although in the past he had often gone away to camp for a few weeks, it had always been with a friend or with his brother. Now, for the first time in his life he would be away from home entirely on his own—and for almost three months.

## CHAPTER 2

# GOING TO SEA

*June 24, 1959*

*Dear Mom and Dad and Grandma,*

 *By the time you get this card, I'll probably be at sea, for I am going on a six-day cruise on a 65-foot boat called the* Paolina T. *We are going down to Mexico a little way. I am eating dinner at the Wind's for a dollar and a half each night and then eating lunch on board ship. On July 7th I leave on a three-week cruise up to San Francisco on an 85-foot boat, the* Orca. *I caught me a dove-nosed shark about four feet long and a two-and-a-half-foot corbina Monday. I will get a payroll cheque every week, I think. I flipped a coin for the* PT *crew with Jeff. Got to work my time and bed comfortable. I hope everything gets better. Must close for I'm going on a grunion run with somebody here.* [Grunion is a slender silvery fish that spawns in huge numbers along California beaches during spring and summer high tides.]

 *Love, Bob*

*P.S. Nancy is a big square.* □ □ □ [Since Nancy couldn't speak, she would make a square with her hands to tease Bob. It was her way of saying, "Bob, you're a square."]

Ballard's first major cruise of the summer came after several weeks at Scripps doing mundane tasks ashore. And although the *Paolina T* was only a small, sea-going tugboat and its mission nothing more than taking repetitive measurements and gathering samples, he was excited to be going on his first oceanographic cruise. During its week at sea, the *Paolina T* followed a predictable routine, steaming back and forth along a series of parallel lines in an area off the southwest California coast. Every so often, the ship would slow down so that the crew could take water samples and temperatures at various depths. This involved lowering a weighted line strung with a series of bottles. Ballard sometimes got the most difficult and dangerous assignment—standing in the "hero bucket" and attaching the bottles as the line was lowered. The hero bucket is a small platform that extends out from the side of the ship just above water level. Dressed in high boots and yellow oilskin pants and jacket, Ballard would wedge himself against the hero bucket railing as waves crashed over him. Then the winch operator lowered what looked like a big lead wrecking ball (the weight) in his direction. If the winch operator miscalculated, the roll of the ship could send the weight crashing into the hull—or into Ballard. Once the ball was in the water, things got easier and Ballard only had to worry about the waves that sometimes came up to his waist as he snapped each sample bottle in place.

After the *Paolina T* returned to La Jolla, Ballard had only a few days on shore before beginning the major cruise of his summer on the *Orca*. The *Orca* was larger than the *PT*, but still an awfully long way from an ocean liner. It was to undertake a similar data-gathering expedition, only this time off the California coast north of San Francisco.

For the first few days the *Orca* sailed north along the coast of California. Near Santa Barbara it put in to port so the crew could enjoy some shore leave. As the junior person on board, Ballard's job was to row the little dinghy that shuttled sailors back and forth between ship and shore.

Most of the men he rowed back to the ship later that night were roaring drunk. Back on board an argument developed between the winch operator and the cook, whose name was Frank.

Frank had very poor eyesight and wore thick glasses. The argument soon turned into a shoving match. Then the winch operator knocked Frank's glasses onto the deck and broke them. The enraged cook groped his way back to the kitchen and returned to the mess brandishing a meat cleaver and swearing he would kill the winch operator. Ballard and every other person in the room knew that without his glasses the cook was virtually blind. There was no telling where that meat cleaver might end up. Ballard only remembers jumping up to grab hold of a light fixture and then finding himself hanging from the ceiling. Meanwhile several crewmen managed to overpower Frank before he did any damage.

The rest of the cruise up the coast passed uneventfully.

But after putting into San Francisco for some brief shore leave, the *Orca* headed out to sea—and into one of the worst storms to batter the California coast in many years. When the storm hit, the winch operator was thrown from his bunk, slammed into a post, and broke his hip. The weather got so bad, all the captain could do was head into the wind and ride out the storm while someone on board who knew a little first aid gave the injured man some morphine. The ship radioed for help, and the U.S. Coast Guard promised to send out a vessel to pick up the hurt crew member.

The rough weather on the *Paolina T* was nothing compared to what the *Orca* now encountered. For three days, the small ship battled raging winds and huge swells. The sensation, which soon loses its thrill, is something like an endless ride on a roller coaster. Riding up each swell seems like climbing a small mountain. At the peak there's a moment when the ship seems to hang suspended, before plunging with a gut-wrenching lurch into the next trough. The best way to live through the ordeal is to find a sheltered spot on deck, make your mind a blank, and try to sleep.

Not everyone coped equally well. A wealthy graduate student from Berkeley, on board as part of his studies, spent each day of the storm wearing his life jacket and sitting motionless in one of the lifeboats. But Ballard, although he didn't exactly enjoy the experience, felt good about simply surviving (and not being sick). Although the sway of the ship was worst on the bridge, which is high above a vessel's center of gravity, he even

24

enjoyed going up to visit the captain and looking out over the endless range of watery mountaintops. He was up there the day the Coast Guard cutter was due to arrive, watching for it through a pair of field glasses. How it would manage to come alongside and take off the injured winch operator, he couldn't imagine.

When he finally spotted the Coast Guard ship plowing in from the east, it looked incredibly tiny and helpless as it rose and fell on the gigantic swells that rose even higher than the top of the ship itself. Then, all of a sudden, a towering wave, twice the height of the average swell, came out of nowhere and swallowed up the cutter. Ballard didn't have time to wonder about the other ship's fate. The same wave was heading directly toward the *Orca*, coming right for the bridge.

He can remember that moment now as if it were happening all over again. A massive wall of water—like the pictures he'd seen of tidal waves—crashed down on his fragile ship. He still can't believe that the top of the wave was as high as the bridge he was standing on. When it hit, it blew out the bridge windows, took out the portholes in the galley, and almost sank the ship. Ballard and the others on the bridge narrowly escaped serious injury from the flying glass. The engine room flooded. One crew member had his leg broken by a flying chunk of heavy porthole glass.

Miraculously, the Coast Guard cutter also survived the attack of this rogue wave. A rogue wave is a freak wave formed when many small waves accidentally combine. But the rescue ship still couldn't get close enough to the *Orca* to take off the injured crew members. For the next two days the ships rode out the storm together. When the weather finally broke, the *Orca* limped into the northern California port of Eureka. Its hull was badly damaged, its engine nearly ruined, and everyone on board desperately in need of a rest.

Ballard was probably relieved to learn that the last month of his Scripps summer would be spent on land, working at a research station on the Pacific coast of Baja California, about eighty-five miles south of San Diego. The station was in the charge of a senior Scripps scientist named Carl Hubbs, a sixty-five-year-old marine biologist who was an expert on the California gray whale.

On the appointed day, Ballard showed up at Dr. Hubbs's office. The older man sized him up from behind thick glasses, then greeted him gruffly. Without further formalities, he said, "Let's go." Before Ballard had time to catch his breath, his luggage was loaded in the back of Hubbs's Jeep and they were flying southward, seemingly without regard for speed limits or traffic signs.

Dr. Hubbs said little until the Jeep crossed the Mexican border. Then he barked out, "Have you got your tourist visa?" No one had mentioned to Ballard that such a document was required, and he admitted that he had not. In those days, there were no checkpoints at the border itself. It was only once you traveled south of the border town of Tijuana that the Mexican authorities would stop your car and demand identification. Such a checkpoint was just up ahead.

Without warning, Hubbs turned the steering wheel sharply, the Jeep jerked off the road, and Ballard found himself being driven at full speed through a cornfield. The Jeep bounced and jolted as cornstalks rushed by at eye level. Once Hubbs had driven around the checkpoint, he returned to the highway and continued on to the tiny fishing village of Punta Banda, where the research station was located.

At Punta Banda, Dr. Hubbs came and went with dizzying suddenness and unpredictability. Sometimes Ballard was the only person at the station. At other times there would be several scientists or graduate students conducting experiments. Through it all, Ballard had two main responsibilities. One was to take wind measurements several times a day from the top of the hill where the tent camp was located. The other was to row out each day to the little boat anchored just offshore. The boat held a machine that recorded the water temperature in the cold water upwelling that was the focus of Dr. Hubbs's studies.

Compared to the hearty food Ballard had eaten on board ship, the meals at Punta Banda were awful—mostly canned military rations. When Ballard attempted to add to this fare with fresh fish he had caught, Hubbs insisted on pickling them in formaldehyde and taking them back to his lab for study. One day he noticed Ballard drinking from one of the large glass bottles marked "Arrowhead Distilled Water."

"What are you doing?" he demanded.

"Well, I'm drinking this water," Ballard replied. "What's wrong with that?"

"It's not distilled water, that's what's wrong," Hubbs told him. "That's from the local water supply. We use it to refill the radiator in the Jeep."

Before Ballard could fully digest this unsettling information, Hubbs had disappeared again, off to chase gray whales or some other underwater fascination. This time Ballard was completely by himself. And he grew gravely ill with dysentery.

Barely able to move or breathe and in excruciating pain, he lay for several days in the choking heat of his tent. No one came to visit. It seemed that he was completely alone in the world. He recalls this ordeal now as one of the worst nightmares of his life. "At first I was afraid I was going to die. Then, as the pain got worse, I was afraid I wasn't going to die," he says. He became severely dehydrated and at times delirious. Looking back, it seems a small miracle he lived to tell the tale— or that he ever went near an oceanographer again.

Returning to his senior year at Downey High School must have seemed like a return from a trip to the moon. And for whatever reason, things suddenly started to go wrong for Ballard. After making the varsity football team, he suffered a serious concussion that put him off the squad for the season. By winter he had recovered enough to make the varsity basketball team as a forward. But early in the season he landed poorly from a jump, tearing the ligaments in both his

*(Above) In the summer of 1959, Ballard reeled in these tuna from the deck of the* Orca. *That September he returned to Downey High to star on the football team (right). In the winter he took his girlfriend, Diane Hinman, to the Sweetheart Ball (below).*

ankles. He spent the rest of the season on crutches. That spring his tennis comeback ended when he broke an ankle. Worst of all, his brother, Dick, who was now in his second year at the University of California at Berkeley and majoring in physics, developed a serious intestinal illness known as Crohn's Disease. For a time it seemed as though Dick might die. He ultimately had to leave school for a year, but returned to complete his college degree.

Ballard's grades were good enough to assure him admittance to the University of California, the question now was which campus. Berkeley was out. There was no way he was going to start competing all over again with his brother's reputation. More and more he was drawn to the University of California at Santa Barbara.

During the *Orca* cruise the previous summer, his ship had spent a day with a number of science students and professors from the Santa Barbara area. One of these was a geology professor at Santa Barbara named Robert Norris. Ballard had been impressed with Norris and took him up on his invitation to come and see him at the university. He liked what he saw, applied, and was accepted.

And so, in September 1960, eighteen-year-old Bob Ballard packed his bags, said good-bye to his girl-friend, Diane, and headed off to college. He and Diane promised to be faithful. But he was rapidly leaving Downey and his life there behind.

# CHAPTER 3

# SCIENTIST IN TRAINING

IN EARLY SEPTEMBER 1960, BOB BALLARD ARRIVED ON the campus of the University of California at Santa Barbara to begin his freshman year. UC Santa Barbara was a medium-sized but fast-growing liberal arts college of slightly fewer than four thousand undergraduates. (By the time Ballard graduated four-and-a-half years later, the student population had more than doubled.) The setting was beautiful—rugged cliffs overlooking the Pacific Ocean. Classes were small, the faculty was mostly young and enthusiastic, and students received a lot of individual attention.

Ballard dove into campus life with gusto. He played freshman basketball, joined Sigma Alpha Epsilon (one of the most popular fraternities on campus), and became active in student government. As well, he took on a heavy academic load, enrolling in the physical sciences program. This was a combined major in physics, math, chemistry, and geology— almost like taking four majors at once. What with the other freshman academic requirements, including a foreign language and English literature, he found his first year somewhat overwhelming. He remembers being terrified that he would flunk out. He didn't.

Robert Norris, the professor Ballard had met when the *Orca* put into Santa Barbara, taught Ballard's first year Physical Geology course. Norris remembers the eighteen-year-old freshman as someone with an out-going—even brash—personality, a young man who was hard to ignore. He was bright, but unfocused. "Ballard could do so many things well," Dr. Norris says, "that he found it difficult to channel his energies." Which made it all the more surprising that the young man carried with him a sense of inferiority compared to his father or his older brother. When Norris learned this he counseled Ballard to rid himself of the notion. "I told him he didn't have to play second fiddle to anybody." Norris, whose special interest was marine geology, became an important mentor figure.

One ritual of Santa Barbara undergraduate life would seem strange at most American universities today. Every Thursday morning all the freshman and sophomore men, along with many juniors and seniors, donned U.S. Army uniforms and spent several hours drilling in the Reserve Officer Training Corps. Because the University of California was on land donated by the federal government, its male students were obligated to pay back this gift in the form of ROTC service. Ballard didn't mind this obligation. In fact, he loved it.

He became a dedicated cadet. In his senior year he was deputy brigade commander of the Santa Barbara unit. At Santa Barbara Ballard began to question some of the beliefs he'd grown up with, including his religion. His mother had raised the family as church-going Lutherans, like her own mother. During a philosophy course he learned about the theory of existentialism and became interested in the writings of the famous French existentialist philosopher Jean-Paul Sartre. Sartre believed that human beings are masters of their own destinies. They can't blame anyone or anything else for their problems and they are responsible for their own actions. This philosophy appealed to the young Ballard, who liked to think of himself as marching to the beat of a drummer only he could hear. He interpreted it to mean that any obstacle could be overcome, if you had the will.

In Ballard's junior year—1962-1963—his busy life-style almost became too much. He was president of his junior class, playing intramural sports, earning outstanding ROTC cadet honors, and dating a coed named Lana Rose. Something had to give—and it did. His grades were suffering. He realized that if he wanted to get into graduate school, he would need to become more serious about his studies.

In senior year things became serious in more ways than one. He and Lana became engaged to be married. He spent more and more time in the library and less time partying at the fraternity house. After Christmas, he applied to the Scripps Institution of Oceanography for graduate school, and in the spring they called him down for an interview.

He was interviewed by Dr. Fred Spiess, then dean of the graduate program. In 1964 Spiess was already one of the pioneers of underwater science, a former nuclear physicist who had invented FLIP, a long cigar-shaped platform that flipped into a vertical position while in the water. This allowed scientists in the submerged half to study sound waves underwater. It would have been a dream come true for Ballard to return to Scripps and study with Spiess. But it was not to be. A few weeks after the interview, he received a letter telling him he'd been turned down. Judging from Professor Norris's letter of recommendation, it is easy to see why. "He is as personable a student as we have had in this department," wrote Norris, "But more than once I have been annoyed because of his failure to apply himself to academic affairs as intensively as he should." According to Norris, the "gay social whirl" still occupied too much of Ballard's time.

Ballard was devastated. Up until this point in his life, he had enjoyed a lot of success and very few failures. The football concussion and other sports injuries during his senior year of high school were disappointments, but they hadn't destroyed his self-confidence. This was different. If Scripps didn't want him, maybe he wasn't cut out for scientific work. He began to question his ability—and to doubt his dream of becoming an explorer under the ocean.

His self-doubt edged toward despair when Lana

informed him she had decided to break off their engagement. His sense of rejection deepened and the self-questioning increased. Ballard entered what he now refers to as an "identity crisis." When he returned home that summer, he signed up for business and accounting classes at UCLA. If he wasn't cut out for oceanography, maybe he should be thinking about a career in business. But after talking it over with his parents, he decided to give oceanography one more try.

By taking summer courses Ballard had earned enough credits to shorten the usual five-year program into four-and-a-half. That final semester at Santa Barbara had an eerie, unreal quality for Ballard. Almost all his friends had graduated the previous June. "I felt like a ghost," he recalls. "I was there, but I was invisible." Very much out of character, he kept to himself, focusing on his studies. Meanwhile he applied to the graduate program at the University of Hawaii Department of Oceanography and was accepted. The idea of going to Hawaii appealed to him. It was about as far away as he could get from the rejections he had recently experienced.

In January 1965, he graduated from the University of California, Santa Barbara, with a bachelor's degree in physical science. A few days later he hopped on a plane to Honolulu.

Before Ballard left for Hawaii, Professor Norris told him to look up his brother, Kenneth. Dr. Kenneth Norris, then a biology professor at UCLA, was also the director of the Oceanic Institute just outside of Honolulu. Ballard would need a job to support himself through grad school. Maybe Ken Norris could give him one.

The day after Ballard arrived in Hawaii, he rented a Honda motorcycle and rode out to Makapuu Point, fifteen miles from Honolulu on the north coast of the island of Oahu, where the Oceanic Institute was located. The little motorbike had to be pushed up the steeper hills. The Hawaiian sun was hot, and Ballard began to wonder if the whole thing was worth it.

He found the Institute, walked into the office, and asked to see Dr. Norris. But Norris was away on a research trip. However the head research trainer at Sea Life Park was willing to talk to him. Sea Life Park was the money-making arm of the Oceanic Institute. Its aquarium and daily trained-porpoise shows packed in the tourists, providing about two thirds of the money needed for the institute's biological ocean research.

The head trainer introduced herself as Karen Pryor. "Have you ever worked with large animals?" she asked him. She had already been impressed by the young man's smooth manner. He would be ideal to work as a narrator for the daily shows at Sea Life Park—as long as he could also get along with the porpoises.

"Sure, with horses," he replied. During junior high in Downey, Ballard had had a job at a local riding stable.

"Come with me."

Karen found Ballard a pair of swimming trunks, told him to put them on, then led him to the porpoise-training tank. He could see a number of the animals in the water, darting and playing.

"Jump in," she told him.

He looked at her for a moment, then did as she instructed. The porpoises didn't come near him.

"You've got yourself a job," Karen Pryor said. Ballard had proved he wasn't afraid of the animals and that was enough for her.

The next day Ballard registered for classes at the University of Hawaii and arranged a schedule that wouldn't conflict with his job at Sea Life Park. That afternoon he reported for work as an apprentice porpoise trainer and show narrator. Porpoises, or dolphins, are really small whales with teeth. (Although some scientists distinguish between porpoises and dolphins, more often the two words are used interchangeably.) Like whales, they are warm-blooded mammals who can't breathe underwater. In the mid-sixties, very little was known about these intelligent creatures.

At the beginning Ballard worked with spotted dolphins who had already been trained to do various stunts such as jumping through hoops or over a series of bars. As he puts it, "The dolphins trained me." Then he graduated to helping train porpoises that had been recently captured at sea. This is a real art, that requires great skill, patience, and ultimately love.

Dolphin training involves a series of stages, each

one more complex than the one before. The trainer begins by getting the animal to understand that each time a whistle is blown, it will be rewarded with a fish. Then the dolphin learns to perform a simple behavior—perhaps jumping out of the water—for a food reward. Gradually these behaviors can be "shaped" into complicated actions, like playing volleyball before an amazed audience of tourists.

Karen Pryor's instinct had been right. Ballard turned out to be good at hosting shows at Sea Life Park's Hawaii Ocean Theater. He quickly learned how to use jokes to hold people's attention and to make scientific information easier to digest. But the most interesting and challenging part of Ballard's work with porpoises was his job as a research assistant for Ken Norris, who was then training these animals for experiments in the open ocean.

Before Ballard arrived on the scene, Norris had already conducted open-ocean trials to test how fast a porpoise can swim. His test animal was a bottle-nose porpoise named Keiki. Keiki, which means "child" in Hawaiian, had been captured while still a teenager and proved an unusually cooperative and trainable individual. He adopted his trainers as family and would do anything to please them. Although the final tests were performed in the open ocean, he always returned when called. And he proved what Dr. Norris had suspected. Dolphins can't swim as fast as many people, who'd watched them seeming to outrace speeding ships, believed. Keiki's top speed was only fourteen

*To help pay his way through school in Hawaii, Ballard took a job training porpoises and hosting shows (above) at Sea Life Park. He also trained Makapuu (left), one of the first False Killer Whales ever held in captivity.*

39

knots. There are species that can swim as fast as twenty-three knots, but the only way a dolphin can keep up with a fast ship is by surfing in its wake.

After the speed trials, Keiki learned to assist scuba diving teams, for instance, carrying bottom samples to a surface vessel and even taking messages from the ship to divers working below. He was a truly remarkable animal.

Around the time Ballard began helping Norris, the biologist had just suffered a serious setback. His second subject for open-ocean release was a female rough-tooth porpoise named Pono. Pono ("justice" in Hawaiian) was one of the first of the species *Steno bredanensis* to be taken alive. Stenos are actually rather ugly as dolphins go, with long snouts lined with stubby pointed teeth and bodies pockmarked with round, pink scars caused by attacks from tiny cookie-cutter sharks.

Ugly, perhaps, but definitely very smart—and choosy about their friends. Pono's chief trainer, Dotty Samson, quickly developed such a close relationship with her that the porpoise would actually let Samson walk on her back, sinking to the bottom of the training tank rather than protesting this apparent indignity. The two would swim and play together; Pono would allow Dotty Samson to "ride" her by holding onto her dorsal fin. But she didn't like everyone. She completely rejected one male trainer who used harsh methods. Pretty soon, whenever this fellow appeared at her tank Pono would rise out of the water and try to grab him with her sharp teeth. As a result he had to be given other responsibilities.

Finally Pono was ready for the experiments Dr. Norris wanted to conduct. Almost nothing was then known about a porpoise's diving ability. How deep could these air-breathing sea mammals go? And how many dives a day could they handle?

Pono had been taught to dive each time Dotty Samson put her hand on the porpoise's forehead and took it away. Pono would then immediately plunge almost straight down to a contraption made up of a lever and a waterproof doorbell. Her job was to press the lever. When the doorbell rang she knew she had completed the task successfully. At the same moment a light flashed on board ship, telling Dr. Norris she had made it to the test depth.

After each dive, the lever was lowered, until it was over 125 feet deep. By the afternoon of the experiments Pono had made over fifty dives and showed no sign of tiring. (Subsequent research showed that some dolphins can make hundreds of dives in a single day and regularly reach depths of a thousand feet or more.) As the experiments continued after lunch, Pono suddenly became very nervous, circling the ship in wider circles and refusing to answer her recall signal. Then someone noticed shadowy flickers in the water below. Sharks had been attracted by the buzz of her doorbell. Pono was terrified.

Despite all Pono's training, nothing Dr. Norris or Dotty Samson tried could lure Pono back to the boat.

Gradually the porpoise drew farther and farther away until she disappeared entirely. Samson was heartbroken. She felt as though she had just lost a good friend.

If Dr. Norris was going to continue his experiments, another porpoise was needed quickly. He and Karen Pryor chose two animals, a mature male roughtooth named Kai ("Ocean") and a juvenile roughtooth female named Hou ("Happy"). Hou would be trained as a backup in case Kai also escaped.

This is where Bob Ballard entered the story. He took a major part in training Hou, spending many hours working with her in the training tank, and developing a deep bond with the animal. She was timid and slow to learn. But when the series of experiments with Kai began, it didn't look as though Hou would be needed. Ballard was part of the team scheduled to work with Kai over a ten-day period in the waters of Pokai Bay. Each morning he was the one who got in the cage attached to the side of the boat and put on Kai's harness. Dr. Norris recalls him as being fearless about this sort of thing.

Over the next five days, Kai made nearly three hundred dives. To make sure sharks would not be attracted, the doorbell buzzer was replaced with a hoop. When Kai swam through the hoop, he broke a light beam. This sent a signal to the surface. The whole series of tests was covered by a photographer and a writer from *Life* magazine. Dr. Norris's experiments were beginning to attract popular interest. Then, late on the afternoon of the fifth day, Kai decided he had simply had enough. Here is how Karen Pryor describes what happened next in her book, *Lads Before the Wind*: "He looked at the hoop, at the cage, and at us; and then he took off, headed for the horizon, leaping and chasing flying fish ahead of him as he went, a wild animal who had suddenly chosen to be free."

No one was upset by Kai's decision, but suddenly meek little Hou was expected to take over. The next morning Ballard drove back to Sea Life Park to get her. She was small enough that he could pick her up in his arms and carry her to the station wagon, where he gently placed her in her specially constructed stretcher. It's actually easier on a dolphin to travel by road than on a boat, where the rolling of the vessel makes the journey very uncomfortable. When Ballard reached Pokai Bay, he created a small sensation as he carried Hou through the parking lot to the research ship.

Unlike Kai, Hou proved a very reluctant participant in Dr. Norris's experiments. When her cage was being towed out to the test site, she wouldn't swim along. She allowed herself to bang up against the bars. To prevent her from hurting herself, the crew was forced to carry her on deck. Despite all Ballard's training, that day she would perform only a few dives and seemed to tire easily. On the second day, she caught a cold and Dr. Norris decided to call off the experiments. Contrary to her name, Hou was not a happy dolphin.

That evening back at Sea Life Park, Ballard returned Hou to the tank and got in the water to comfort her. To his amazement, she attacked him, butting him hard—but not biting him. In an instant he realized that his friend was angry, that she blamed him for what she had suffered over the past two days.

Hou's ordeal wasn't Ballard's fault, but he found this rejection as painful as if a person he loved had turned on him. Perhaps they had pushed Hou too hard. Perhaps she wasn't ready for the experiments. The experience with Hou ruined dolphin work for Ballard. He quit Sea Life Park and found work in a local dive shop. He never helped train dolphins again.

Hou, however, went on to become something of a star. In later experiments Karen Pryor conducted to explore animal creativity, Hou and another dolphin proved that porpoises can learn to come up with new behaviors on their own and become more independent as a result. Hou went from being a rather sad and retiring creature to a strong and self-confident individual.

Meanwhile Ballard had met and fallen for "the girl next door." Actually, she lived across the street from his Honolulu apartment and worked in a nearby flower shop, saving money to continue a trip around the world. Her name was Marjorie Hargas. Her family came from Montana, but she had grown up in Florida. Ballard, too, had been born in the Midwest, in Wichita, Kansas, before his family moved to the coast. After she met Ballard, Marjorie gave up the idea of continuing her travels.

Then, in the late spring of 1966, with Ballard's graduate studies only partly complete, he got an offer he couldn't refuse. It came in the form of a letter from Andy Rechnitzer, director of North American Aviation's recently formed ocean systems department. Ballard had worked there during the summer between his freshman and sophomore years. Andy's letter offered him a job helping develop a deep-submergence vehicle to be called the *Beaver Mark IV*. The twenty-five-foot-long sub was designed to take divers working on ocean-drilling rigs to and from work. If Ballard accepted, North American would not only pay his moving expenses, but also pay his tuition while he completed his graduate studies at the University of Southern California.

The only doubt in Ballard's mind was whether Marjorie would come with him. He proposed marriage, she accepted, and they were married in July 1966 in Long Beach, California, the Los Angeles suburb where his parents now lived. He was twenty-four years old, with a good job and excellent career prospects. Life was good. The horizon looked cloudless.

Then, one day early in 1967, an officer in a U.S. Navy uniform knocked on Ballard's door, handed him a formal-looking document, and said, "Congratulations. You're in the Navy. You have six days to report for active duty in Boston." Suddenly Ballard's life was turned upside-down.

While at graduate school in Hawaii, he had transferred from the army reserve into the naval reserve. But the Navy's paperwork hadn't fully caught up with his move to California. Although he was still in

45

school, the Navy thought he wasn't. At the time, he didn't know enough to argue the case. Besides, the Vietnam War was at its height and lots of young men were being drafted.

It could have been much worse. His active-duty posting was to the Office of Naval Research in Boston, Massachusetts. There he would act as the liaison officer with various scientific research programs being funded by the Navy. At the beginning of March, he and Marjorie packed up their few belongings, hopped in their car, and drove east. Taped beneath the dashboard was a check for one thousand dollars, their life savings. It was the first time Ballard had been east of the Mississippi to what he imagined was the stuffy, old world of New England. But for him this old world would prove to be the gateway to a new frontier.

# CHAPTER 4

# THE AQUANAUT

AS SCIENTIFIC LIAISON OFFICER FOR THE OFFICE OF Naval Research (ONR) in Boston, Bob Ballard quickly made an imprint on the New England oceanographic community. In particular, he made an impression at the Woods Hole Oceanographic Institution—WHOI for short—in the town of Falmouth located at the base of the Cape Cod peninsula. Ballard's job was to keep an eye on all the scientific research being funded by the Navy in New England. Well over half of these projects were at Woods Hole, whose only rival in the world of American underwater science at the time was Scripps.

Because of Woods Hole's importance, ONR kept an office there, where Ballard spent two or three days each week. He quickly learned his way around, and he liked what he saw. The Institution was beautifully situated on wooded acres overlooking Vineyard Sound with the island of Martha's Vineyard floating in the distance. And in the late sixties it was already home to many of the leading minds in the still-young science of oceanography. Kenneth O. Emery (K. O. for short) was one of these.

Ballard immediately hit it off with this man more than twice his age who was one of the leading marine geologists of his day. It helped that they had a few things in common. For example, Emery had taught marine geology at the University of Southern California—where Ballard had been enrolled in the graduate program before his sudden move to Boston. They also shared a belief that submarines should be used in oceanographic research. Almost as soon as Emery met Ballard, he asked him when he was going to finish his Ph.D. Although Ballard was busy with his Navy job, Emery saw to it that the young man not only participated in some of his scientific work but received some of the credit. For instance, he invited Ballard to help him write two scientific papers on their research expeditions.

The other attraction of Woods Hole was a funny-looking contraption called *Alvin*. This compact, three-person research submarine, which had lived at WHOI since its completion in 1964, had already made world headlines—but not for scientific reasons. In 1966 a U.S. Air Force B-52 carrying four hydrogen bombs collided in midair with a tanker airplane over the Mediterranean coast of Spain, and dropped its cargo. The bombs weren't armed, so none exploded; but one fell into the sea. After a two-month search involving a small fleet of surface ships and two submarines (*Aluminaut* was the other), *Alvin* found the bomb and it was safely brought back to the surface.

*Alvin* was named in honor of Woods Hole oceanographer Allyn Vine, who had fought long and hard for its construction. The tiny submarine was about as far away from Ballard's romantic conception of Jules Verne's *Nautilus* as you could get. It was pint-sized and tubby-looking. A writer in the *New York Times* once called it "a chewed-off cigar with a helmet." In later years a more streamlined outer hull improved *Alvin*'s looks.

But appearances weren't the point. *Alvin* was the first deep-diving submarine built exclusively for scientists. The earlier bathyscaph ("deep ship")—the type of submersible that had pioneered deep-sea diving for science—was built by the French balloonist Auguste Piccard in 1948. It could dive deeper than *Alvin*, but was big and slow and awkward and had only one tiny window. *Alvin*'s specially engineered six-foot-wide steel "personnel sphere" permitted it to dive safely to depths of six thousand feet—enough to allow it to visit about half of the ocean floor. Its three Plexiglas viewports permitted the crew to make close observations of their surroundings. And its mechanical arm had a pincerlike claw on the end that could gather samples, then deposit them in a basket in front of the sub for examination at the surface.

Ballard found *Alvin* fascinating, and he quickly made friends with the Alvin Group, the close-knit team of Woods Hole scientists and technicians who cared for the sub and took it to sea. Head of the group was William Rainnie, a former Navy submariner who'd originally been hired as *Alvin*'s first pilot. In Bill Rainnie, Ballard found his other Woods Hole mentor. During late night sessions with K. O. Emery and another close colleague, Al Uchupi, he could talk pure science and speculate on the geological secrets still hidden in the deep sea. With Rainnie, he could talk technology and dream of deeper dives and more sophisticated submersibles.

One of the things he and Rainnie talked about was when Ballard would get his first opportunity to dive in *Alvin*. Then, on October 16, 1968, it suddenly seemed as though talking was as close as Ballard would get. At the beginning of *Alvin* dive number 308, the sub was being lowered into the sea from its mother ship, the *Lulu*. Two crew members were already inside; the third stood in the "sail," the fiberglass housing above the sphere's single entry hatch. Suddenly the sub's nose plunged forward. Two of the cables holding its cradle had snapped, and *Alvin* was about to disappear into the sea. Somehow, the two men inside managed to escape as water poured into the open hatchway. But *Alvin* was gone, lost in fifty-two hundred feet of water.

It took almost a year before *Alvin* was found, raised, and brought back to land. It was more than another year before she was ready to go to sea again. Amazingly, the crew's lunch of apples and bologna sandwiches was still edible after ten months marinating in deep-sea brine; this led biologists to discover that bacteria works much more slowly at great depths.

As a result of this mishap, Ballard's first dive in a deep submersible didn't take place in *Alvin*. It came on December 4, 1969, when he joined K. O. Emery on a research trip in a sub called the *Ben Franklin*. The *Ben Franklin* was a submarine specially designed to drift for days below the surface of the Gulf Stream, carried along by this greatest of all the "rivers in the sea." It was named after Franklin because he was the first person to conduct a scientific study of the Gulf Stream. On its first major voyage, the sub drifted for a month from Florida to Nova Scotia without ever coming up for air.

As deep-diving research submersibles go, the *Ben Franklin* was a four-star hotel. There was a kitchen, a shower, even an observation lounge—it made Ballard think of Captain Nemo's *Nautilus*. Its eight bunks, each with its own porthole, were six feet, six inches long— long enough to comfortably handle the bulk of Auguste Piccard's son, Jacques, the sub's designer. The *Ben Franklin* was a "mesoscaph," designed to spend long stretches of time at moderate depths. But Ballard's first dive in it, off West Palm Beach, was merely an overnighter to a maximum depth of nine hundred feet.

The hot Florida sun beat down on the six men as they climbed through the *Ben Franklin's* two hatches and into the stuffy interior. Once the hatches were closed, chemical scrubbers kept the air breathable but it never lost a slightly medicinal smell. The pilot signaled the support ship that all systems checked out, then the tow rope was released and water pumped into the ballast tanks, causing the fifty-foot-long vessel to begin its descent. Glued to a porthole, Ballard watched in utter fascination as the water began to darken. A few colorful fish swam lazily by. Then, out of nowhere, a big sailfish charged toward his viewport, banging its sword with a clanging thud against the metal hull. The dangerous-looking fish soon gave up its vain attack on this giant trespasser and swam away. Calm returned, and in a few minutes the last light was gone. Even at these modest depths the *Ben Franklin* had entered a region of eternal darkness.

That night the submersible sat gently on the sandy bottom as the Gulf Stream raced silently overhead. The other crew members, who'd been down before, had all turned in, but Ballard couldn't fall asleep. Quietly, he left his bunk and made his way to the sphere-shaped observation lounge in the bow. He sat by one of the windows until dawn, staring into the submarine blackness, reliving his childhood fantasies and dreaming of the future.

While Ballard yearned to do more diving in research subs, he continued to explore his passion for scuba diving. Soon after his arrival on the East Coast, he had joined the legendary Boston Sea Rovers, one of the oldest diving clubs in the world. At club meetings he met a unique combination of amateur diving enthusiasts and professional scientists and explorers. Its annual convention attracted some of the biggest names in the underwater world—people like Eugenie

Clark, the marine biologist famous for her work with sharks, and Jacques-Yves Cousteau, who had invented the Aqua-lung and developed the diving saucer (*coupe plongeante*), a two-person submersible designed to work at depths up to a thousand feet. Many were serious scientists who weren't afraid of popularizing their work. Some of them even dreamed of visiting famous sunken shipwrecks. The most famous wreck of all, everyone agreed, was the *Titanic*. The wreck of the lost passenger ship was known to lie in water about thirteen thousand feet deep, a little more than twice *Alvin's* limit. Too bad *Alvin* couldn't dive that deep, Ballard thought.

When Bob Ballard and his wife, Marjorie, first arrived in Massachusetts, they decided to live in Cohasset, a coastal town about halfway between his Boston and Woods Hole offices. Ballard's Navy salary was small, and the young couple lived frugally. (On his way to and from Woods Hole he would always stop at Otis Air Force Base to shop in the subsidized PX store.) The family budget became even tighter in July 1968, when their first son, Todd, was born. But at least Ballard's job seemed secure. He expected his Navy appointment to last the usual three years, from March 1967 to March 1970. Then, in September 1969, his commanding officer informed him that budget restraints caused by the Vietnam War meant the Navy was reducing its payroll. Ballard could either become a career Navy man or he would be released from duty at the end of the month.

Ballard didn't want to spend the rest of his career in the U. S. Navy, but he had no idea how to support his family while he completed his graduate studies and gained his Ph.D. However, thanks to his two Woods Hole mentors, the problem was quickly solved. K. O. Emery arranged for him to enter the graduate program in oceanography at the nearby University of Rhode Island. And Bill Rainnie offered him a job finding funding for *Alvin*.

This was ironic, since until then Ballard's job had involved Navy funding of *Alvin*'s scientific work. But Navy money was drying up, and Ballard had recently been telling Rainnie he'd better start looking elsewhere for funds. "You've got such great ideas," Rainnie was now saying, "Let's see you put them into practice."

There seems no question that Bob Ballard was a fountain of schemes and proposals. In *Water Baby*, Victoria Kaharl's exhaustive history of the Alvin Group, she has this to say about the young Californian. "The ideas seemed to gush from the twenty-eight-year-old Ballard. He was brash and cocky, but serious and convincing." Ballard couldn't resist Rainnie's challenge. It appealed to the salesman and showman in his makeup—his grandfather May would have understood. And according to Kaharl, he proved to be the right man for the job. "The 1971 dive schedule was an unprecedented mishmash of funders, barter, and IOUs—much of it Ballard's handiwork." Such skill at raising money would be useful later in Ballard's career.

For now, however, while salesmanship provided for his growing family—his second son, Douglas, was born in October 1970—Ballard's main focus was science. If he wanted to rise in his chosen profession, he needed that Ph.D. Fortunately he had a clear idea what he wanted to write about: the brand-new theory of plate tectonics.

In the late sixties and early seventies, earth scientists were excited by a revolutionary new theory about how the planet worked. Evidence was mounting that the earth's crust was divided into a number of major plates which moved as if on slow conveyer belts. Although this movement was too slow for human beings to notice, over millions of years it had caused the continents to split apart and separate. And where two plates collided, mountain ranges formed or crust broke off and was swallowed up in deep trenches. Some of the main places where these plates were moving apart were beneath the oceans, places scientists had not yet visited. For an oceanographer, it was a once-in-a-lifetime opportunity, and Bob Ballard seized it.

For his Ph.D., Ballard decided to search the continental shelf beneath the Gulf of Maine for evidence to support this exciting new theory. His research tool would be *Alvin*—now finally back in service—and he would turn himself into a land geologist under water—someone who uses his eyes to gather evidence and draw conclusions. Over the course of twenty-five dives between 1971 and 1973, Ballard peered through *Alvin's* viewports into the murky water and collected rock samples with *Alvin's* mechanical arm. It was uncomfortable work. Even layers of clothing and warm sweaters couldn't take away the chill clamminess in the steel sphere surrounded by near-freezing water. After six or seven hours of work on the bottom, he might have found nothing, or maybe turned up one small clue. The crew got so cold, that when the sub surfaced they would head straight for a steaming hot shower just to warm up.

But Ballard was a determined young man. His will and his energy became legendary, earning him the nickname the White Tornado, after a television commercial about a popular detergent. Following the day's dive, while all but the men on the *Lulu's* night watch had gone to bed, he stayed up to conduct seismic surveys of the ocean floor. This involved firing a big air gun every thirty seconds and waiting for the echo. The sound waves would pass through the soft upper layers and bounce off the hard rock beneath (the sub-bottom), giving Ballard a true picture of the ocean floor. This allowed him to locate spots were the hard bedrock jutted above the sediment, places where *Alvin* could take rock samples.

Late one night, the sound of Ballard's air gun drove one of the *Lulu's* crew members over the edge. The crewman appeared in the control room and threatened to kill the young scientist. Fortunately George Broderson, *Alvin's* crew chief, saw what was happening

*Ballard (left) and his Woods Hole mentor K.O. Emery (right) prepare to board* Alvin *before a dive.*

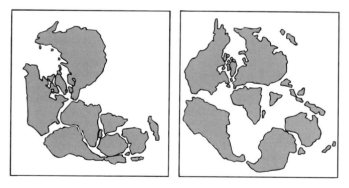

*These illustrations of continental drift show the earth's land masses as they appeared 300 million years ago (above left) and 50 million years ago (above right).*

and came to the rescue. He held the man back, calmed him down, then took him back to his bunk.

Ballard went back to his seismic survey, but decided to get some sleep while doing it. He rigged up a speaker in the lounge and stretched out on a bench. He figured that if the sonic booms stopped, he would wake up. He was just about to nod off when he felt a presence in the room. The same crewman was back, this time wielding a knife. Fortunately Broderson was right behind him and managed to pry the weapon from his hand. Ballard finally stopped his survey for the night. But next evening he was back at it again.

In June 1974, Ballard defended his dissertation, "The Behavior of the Gulf of Maine and Adjacent Region During Continental Collision and Subsequent Separation," before his thesis committee at the University of Rhode Island. Underneath the waters off the coast of New England, Ballard had found convincing evidence that hundreds of millions of years earlier Africa had crashed into North America, causing the Appalachian Mountains to form. Then the two continents had slowly pulled apart, leaving the landscape we know today. Even though some members of the committee still didn't accept the theory of plate tectonics, they awarded him his doctorate.

A few days later, Dr. Robert D. Ballard left on a scientific expedition that would take human beings to a part of the planet more remote and unknown than the surface of the moon. This was the groundbreaking enterprise known as Project FAMOUS.

# CHAPTER 5

# PROJECT FAMOUS

PROJECT FAMOUS REALLY GOT OFF THE GROUND TWO years earlier—in January 1972—during a symposium at Princeton University. The meeting room was filled with many of the most important names in earth sciences. These experts had gathered to discuss the underwater scientist's equivalent to sending a space capsule to the moon—exploring a piece of a submerged mountain range called the Mid-Ocean Ridge. At forty thousand miles, running beneath the Atlantic, Pacific, and Indian Oceans, it is the longest mountain range on earth.

Everyone in the room agreed on one thing: A successful investigation of the ridge would almost certainly provide the final pieces in the puzzle of the theory of plate tectonics. The Mid-Atlantic Ridge is the Atlantic segment of the Mid-Ocean Ridge. Along its entire length the hard outer crust of the earth is cracking and the vast raftlike plates are moving apart leaving gaps in the ocean floor. But just how did this process of "seafloor spreading" happen? And what secrets did this never-glimpsed landscape hide?

Disagreement came when talk turned to the best way of exploring such a remote region of the planet— a landscape about which less was known than the surface of Mars. Most of the scientists argued that it would be cheaper and more effective to tow cameras and sonar sensors from long cables and to conduct seismic surveys from ships safely patrolling on the surface. Then a tall, slim young man rose to make a presentation about the research submarine *Alvin*. He argued that the best way to really find out what was going on along the ridge was to look at it with human eyes, just the way a geologist does on land. And the only way to do that was to dive in a submarine like *Alvin*, just as he had been doing in his own research.

Bob Ballard was not yet thirty and in January 1972, he was still more than two years away from receiving the Ph.D. that would give him credibility in the scientific world. Yet he had conducted more dives in *Alvin* than any other scientist. He had become one of the few experts in the world on using deep submersibles for underwater mapping. But his arguments were met with open skepticism, even hostility.

When Ballard finished speaking and sat down, a prominent member of the National Academy of Sciences, which was sponsoring the symposium, leapt up and asked, "Mr. Ballard, would you please tell me one piece of significant science a submersible ever had anything to do with?" He spoke in the tone of a professor putting an uppity student in his place.

It was one of the few times anyone has ever seen Ballard speechless. Finally a third voice broke the uncomfortable silence. "There isn't any, because nobody has tried to do any significant science from a submersible." The voice belonged to a young geophysicist at Woods Hole. Although he was stretching the truth, his point was valid. *Alvin* had done a fair bit of serious science, but almost none of it had been published. In the world of science, an experiment hasn't really happened until the results have been written up in a scientific journal.

Now other scientists came to Ballard's defense. They argued that a chance to get a firsthand look at the underwater terrain was simply too tempting to pass up. At the end of the conference, the group had agreed that submersibles like *Alvin* should take part. But not everyone was convinced. That evening one distinguished scientist cornered Ballard and told him, "If you fail, we'll melt *Alvin* down and turn it into titanium paper clips."

The reference to titanium was apt. *Alvin*'s steel sphere was about to be replaced by one made of titanium alloy. Not only is titanium one of the few metals that does not rust, it is both stronger and lighter than steel. The change would more than double *Alvin*'s depth limit of six thousand feet, quite enough for the sub to reach the nine-thousand-foot-deep central rift valley of the Mid-Atlantic Ridge.

Over the next several months the scientists planned

a three-year program of exploration named Project FAMOUS. FAMOUS stood for French-American Mid-Ocean Undersea Study because it would involve both French and American ships, submersibles, and scientists. Canadian and British scientists would also take part. The scientists chose a sixty-square-mile area of ocean about four hundred miles south of the Azores, where they could count on the summer weather being warm and the seas mostly calm.

In the first year, the summer of 1972, the target site was mapped more intensely than any part of the ocean bottom before. In addition to sonar and seismic surveys, deep-towed cameras took thousands of pictures. Ballard had a hand in developing one of the two camera vehicles, Woods Hole's ANGUS (for Acoustically NaviGated Underwater Survey). Jokingly called "the dope on a rope," ANGUS was a steel-framed camera sled towed at the end of a long cable, clicking picture after picture of the seafloor. Only when the sled was recovered many hours later and the film developed, did the scientists at the surface find out whether the cameras had worked. Most of the time they had.

When phase one was complete, the scientists had assembled what one geologist at Woods Hole called "the finest bathymetric charts ever made of a small section of the bottom in the deep ocean." These detailed maps of the ocean floor showed a twenty-mile-long section of the valley that runs along the middle of the Mid-Atlantic Ridge. The target area was marked off by two volcanoes, Mount Venus to the north and Mount Pluto to the south. At a gymnasium in Washington, D.C., a photographic mosaic of this area was laid on the floor, and for several days the scientists walked through a replica of the terrain they would soon explore in person.

The men who would be diving into the Mid-Atlantic rift valley prepared as carefully as did the Apollo astronauts for their first trip to the moon. Some of the submarine pilots and scientists trained on land similar to what was expected far beneath the sea: volcanic areas in Iceland and Hawaii. For all Bob Ballard and the others knew, *Alvin* might come down in the crater of an underwater volcano about to erupt.

On August 2, 1973, the French bathyscaph *Archimède* made the first manned dive into the rift valley. *Archimède* was a bathyscaph built by the French Navy, but modeled closely on the earlier bathyscaphs designed by Auguste Piccard. Given that Piccard started out as a balloonist, it's not surprising that the bathyscaph is like a balloon operating underwater. Its buoyancy comes from a large tank filled with gasoline, which is lighter than water.

On *Archimède*'s first descent into the rift, the current was almost as strong as the bathyscaph's puny engines, but the French geophysicist Xavier Le Pichon, one of those initially skeptical about using submersibles, couldn't take his eyes off the strange and dramatic underwater landscape.

One can imagine Ballard's excitement a few days later when he was picked to become only the second scientist, and the first American, to visit the Mid-Atlantic Ridge. He had come down with a painful throat infection the day before, but mentioned it to no one—there was no way he was going to miss out on being a part of history. It turned out to be a piece of history he would happily have avoided.

Partway through the dive, as Ballard tried to maneuver the mechanical claw to grab a rock sample, the bathyscaph's nose suddenly dropped, throwing the three men off balance. Something had triggered the emergency ballast release, ending the dive and sending the submersible accelerating back toward the surface. But what? When smoke began to fill the tiny cabin, the answer became clear. They had an electrical fire on board!

The deep submersible diver's two worst nightmares are to get stuck underwater—wedged into a crevice or tangled in wreckage—or for electrical problems to knock out the life support system. What's worse, a fire burns up precious oxygen. The three crew members grabbed the mouthpieces attached to the emergency oxygen supply. As long as it worked, they should be fine.

Ballard took a breath, but something seemed to be wrong. The more he breathed, the sicker and dizzier he became. He tried to pull out the mouthpiece, but one of his colleagues pushed it back in, thinking that he was panicking. He hadn't been, but now he was— he felt like he was choking to death. Desperately, he grabbed his throat to signal his distress. The pilot got

*(Left) Ballard working in the research ship the* Lulu *during Project FAMOUS*

*(Below)* Alvin *'s mechanical arm reaches out to collect a sample of rock from the ocean floor.*

the message, noticed that the valve on Ballard's line hadn't been turned on, and quickly released a healing flow of oxygen into Ballard's lungs. The smoke started to burn their eyes, so they all put on scuba-diving masks and waited. And prayed. Would the fire shut down the oxygen supply? An hour later when they reached the surface they were all still breathing.

*Archimède's* seven preliminary dives in 1973 prepared the way for the main event in June 1974, when a small fleet converged on the same empty piece of ocean. Three submersibles—the American sub *Alvin,* the French diving saucer *Cyana,* and *Archimède*—each with its own surface support ship, would together explore every nook and cranny between Mount Venus and Mount Pluto.

Ballard's first dive in 1974 took place on his thirty-second birthday, June 30. And this time he was in the cramped but familiar confines of *Alvin.* The routine was old hat to him now, but he still experienced a sense of wonder each time he entered his "inner space" capsule and began another voyage of discovery.

The most dangerous parts of any dive in *Alvin* come at the start and the finish—as the loss of *Alvin* back in 1969 showed. A cable can snap or heavy seas flood the cabin and drown its occupants. That day the sea was calm and the sun had heated the titanium sphere to a sweltering ninety degrees Fahrenheit as Ballard and his two diving companions, pilot Val Wilson and copilot Larry Shumaker, removed their shoes, gingerly climbed down through the fiberglass sail, and lowered themselves into the tiny spherical cabin. They had to be careful not to rub their clothes against the sides of the hatch, which was heavily greased to ensure a perfect waterproof seal.

Wilson closed the hatch from inside, then Ballard turned on the oxygen tank, their only source of fresh air once they left the surface. The pilot checked the various systems, especially the lithium hydroxide blower that removes poisonous carbon dioxide from the cabin's air.

"Oxygen on, blower running," Wilson reported to the surface controller on the *Lulu*'s bridge.

That was the signal for the *Lulu*'s crew to back *Alvin* out from between the support ship's twin hulls.

"*Lulu*, my hatch is closed, no leaks or grounds, my tracking pinger and underwater phone are on, no joy [echo] on the bottom sounder. Request permission to dive."

"Roger, *Alvin*. You are clear to dive. Present water depth is eighty-seven hundred feet. Good luck."

Outside the sub, crewmen and swimmers released the last lines tethering *Alvin* to the *Lulu*, then the pilot flooded the ballast tanks and the twenty-two-foot-long craft began to sink. The three men inside shifted to make themselves comfortable for the long descent. The pilot sat on a small stool facing the forward viewport and the steering controls. On either side of him, Ballard and Shumaker each half-sat, half-lay in a nest of clothing that they would need as the sub grew colder.

Ballard watched out the port window as a jellyfish drifted past his view—its stinging tentacles couldn't harm him now, he thought. In fact, the only time a sea animal had come close to damaging *Alvin* was a few years earlier when a swordfish attacked the sub during an ascent. Somehow the big fish managed to get its weapon wedged between a viewport and the hull, raising fears it might break the seal and let water in. But *Alvin* had remained pressure-proof and that night the crew of the *Lulu* ate fresh swordfish steaks.

As the sub sank deeper the daylight quickly faded—like a sunset in fast forward—and the water color changed from bright blue to dark blue. In less than fifteen minutes, *Alvin* had reached a depth of twelve hundred feet and total darkness. For the rest of their nearly nine-thousand-foot descent they would be in a world without sun—but not without life—sinking at a maximum rate of one hundred feet per minute.

Now the tension of the launch sequence ebbed away, replaced by a sense of timelessness. Conversation faltered, then faded out as the three men turned to their own thoughts. Later, *Alvin* would be fitted with a tape deck and the sounds of classical music would accompany each long fall to the bottom. The titanium hull cooled quickly, and the temperature inside the sphere dropped rapidly as moisture began to condense on the metal. On his first dive in *Alvin* back in 1971, Ballard thought the moisture came from a leak. The pilot told him to taste one of the droplets. It wasn't salty, and he relaxed. For nearly an

*(Left) Ballard communicates with the team on the* Lulu *while on an* Alvin *descent.*

*(Below) He and other scientists examine a sample retrieved from the ocean floor.*

hour, there was little to do except watch the instruments and wonder what awaited them on the bottom.

Finally a voice boomed over the acoustic telephone. "*Alvin,* this is *Lulu.* Your present position is X 55.6, Y 100.4. We suggest you drive a course of 180 degrees at 50 amps for twenty minutes, to close on your bottom target. Over."

Ballard glanced up at the depth meter—six thousand feet—still a long way to go before the bottom.

"This is *Alvin,*" Wilson responded. "Understand."

At eight thousand feet—about seven hundred feet from the seafloor—the pilot turned on the exterior lights, cameras, data logger, and the sub's own sonar system. Suddenly the swish of the sonar scope changed to a high-pitched ping—indicating the west wall of the rift valley was only five hundred yards away.

Two hundred feet from the seafloor, Wilson dropped two of *Alvin's* descent weights, lightening the sub by five hundred pounds and rapidly slowing its fall. Since the sub would then begin to rise up slowly, the pilot pumped seawater into the six small titanium ballast tanks used to achieve neutral buoyancy. This meant the sub was neither rising nor falling and that the pilot could now "fly" the submarine over the tricky terrain below, using the transponder beacons to pinpoint his position on their underwater map.

Ballard wondered whether the current would be strong, as it was during his dive in *Archimède* the year before. But the underwater wind turned out to be blowing at less than a quarter of a knot, nothing for

*Alvin* to worry about. In fact, Wilson was able to bring the sub down until its nose rested against a steep lava slope near the west wall of the rift. Ballard and Shumaker remained glued to the port and starboard viewports. As *Alvin* explored the surrounding area they saw amazing lava shapes.

There were huge lava piles up to fifteen feet high and thirty feet across, that soon were nicknamed haystacks. Snakelike streams of lava resembled toothpaste squeezed from a tube—these were created as the rapidly cooling surface of a small lava flow hardened while molten rock continued to flow within this pipe. A whole new vocabulary for underwater lava formations would soon be invented—names like trapdoor, cousteau, bread crust, elephant trunk, and swan—to describe these new lava forms.

But today was for reconnoitering the lay of the land, not lava hunting. *Alvin* lifted off and headed east, across the rift valley. Like a helicopter flying just above the treetops, the tiny sub floated over a landscape that spoke of the earth's creation.

"Wow, look at that!"

Out *Alvin's* window Ballard was staring into a twenty-foot-wide fissure in the valley floor, big enough for *Alvin* to enter, but too tight to risk. When Wilson started to move the sub forward, Ballard objected.

"Let's sit here awhile," he suggested.

The pilot set the sub gently down on the edge of the precipice. It was nearly lunchtime and someone broke out the sandwiches.

Ballard's mind, however, was far from his stomach. As he stared into the seemingly bottomless crack in the earth, plate tectonics ceased being an abstract theory and became real and immediate. "It was as if I was sitting on the crack between Africa and America," he later said. It was here that the ocean floor was spreading as the two continents slowly drifted apart.

After lunch, *Alvin* completed its exploration of the rift valley, then headed back toward the surface. If only the doubters could see what he had seen, Ballard thought, no one would question the theory of plate tectonics again.

In the days that followed, *Cyana, Archimède,* and *Alvin* explored this complex landscape of hardened lava flows, steep cliffs, and yawning fissures. When Ballard wasn't in *Alvin,* he joined the control team on *Lulu.* On one such occasion, *Alvin's* pilot reported matter-of-factly that he'd driven the sub into a crack and couldn't get it out. The men on the surface were horrified. What if the sub stayed stuck?

Two tense hours later, the crew managed to work the sub free by rocking it forward and back like a car stuck in a snowdrift. Thankfully, this was the only close call during the two-month-long expedition during which the three subs made a combined total of forty-four dives. It would take years to analyze all the data this intense period of deep-sea exploration had collected. But one thing was clear: Any doubt about the theory of plate tectonics had been laid to rest.

# CHAPTER 6

# DEEPER SECRETS

BACK AT WOODS HOLE, BOB BALLARD BECAME KNOWN for wearing several hats. He now held the rank of assistant scientist, continuing to spend much of his time conducting serious oceanographic research. He had also become a technology junkie. His fascination with ANGUS, the camera sled that had proved so effective at photographing the Mid-Atlantic Ridge, led him to form the ANGUS group. He dreamed of ever more sophisticated underwater robots that would help, and eventually replace, *Alvin*. His third hat was that of scientific popularizer. In this guise, he wrote the first of what would become a series of articles for *National Geographic*. It described a dive in *Alvin* into the mid-Atlantic rift valley.

Some of Ballard's fellow scientists disliked his tendency to seek the limelight and grumbled that his attempts at making science popular trivialized a complex subject. But this didn't deter him in the slightest. His appetite for new ideas and fresh projects seemed bottomless. Around this time he again began to consider the most intriguing scheme of all, the idea of finding and diving down to the *Titanic*.

As he remembered it later, the idea began to take shape after *Alvin* got its new titanium hull, which was soon cleared to a maximum diving depth of 13,124 feet, enough to reach the famous shipwreck—if it could be located. Now he began seriously researching the ship and its fatal maiden voyage. What was known of the wreck's location? How difficult would it be to locate? Had anyone tried to find it before? Ballard floated proposals with different partners and tried to raise money for an expedition. But for the first few years, he couldn't find a backer. Still, Ballard didn't give up. If only he had the money, the rest ought to be easy.

Meanwhile the success of Project FAMOUS led directly to a series of new scientific expeditions designed to study further the geological forces constantly re-shaping the surface of the earth. In 1976 Ballard led an expedition to the Cayman Trough, a great tear in the ocean crust where two plates slide past each other beneath the Caribbean Sea south of Cuba. As *Alvin* sank down past the the canyon walls, he was able to literally travel back many millions of years of geologic time down to a layer normally hidden far beneath the molten mantle, deeper into the earth's crust than any scientists had ever traveled before.

The next year he was back at the Cayman Trough, this time to dive in the bathyscaph *Trieste II*. *Trieste's* pressure sphere was thicker than *Alvin*'s, permitting it to reach the bottom of the Cayman rift valley, almost twenty-one thousand feet below the surface. Since the fire in *Archimède*, Ballard had developed a healthy fear of bathyscaphs. They were slow and unwieldy, but worst of all, they lacked *Alvin*'s escape clause. In a pinch, *Alvin*'s pressure sphere could be separated from its steel frame to shoot up to the surface with the crew. If a bathyscaph's gasoline "balloon" got punctured, however, there was no way for its crew to get home.

The launch for *Trieste II*'s first dive went smoothly. Then the submarine blimp sank toward the floor of the steep-sided underwater valley. One hour passed. Then another. Two and a half hours into the dive it passed the deepest point reached by *Alvin* at 12,200 feet down. Another half mile to go. As the bottom drew near, the pilot prepared to begin releasing ballast. On *Trieste II*, this took the form of small shotgun pellets dropped from a vertical cone. Because of this system, it took the bathyscaph much longer than *Alvin* to slow its descent. The pilot waited. According to the down-looking sonar the bottom was still a good distance away.

Ballard watched out the lone porthole, wondering what new sights awaited them three miles down. Suddenly his field of vision filled with black—the rocky slope of the valley's side was only a few feet away!

"Wall!" he shouted. The pilot immediately began dropping shot. "It's coming, It's coming," Ballard yelled, but the black wall kept charging at him.

The sub slowed slightly, but too little, too late.

Ballard watched in horror as the front of the gasoline-filled "balloon" hit the rock face and bounced along it, making a sickening scraping sound. In an emergency, a bathyscaph's entire ballast can be dropped with the flick of a switch, which means the dive's over. That's what the pilot did now.

The three men in the cabin held their breaths and stared at the depth meter. If the metal-encased gasoline balloon had ruptured, water would gradually flow into its interior, displacing the less dense gasoline. At some point far below the surface, the bathyscaph would slow, stop, and then start to sink again.

The spinning digital readout whirred, then displayed a new depth number. The bathyscaph was rising. It spun again. Still rising. Ballard's stomach was in a knot. Minutes passed. Then an hour, then two. The bathyscaph was still heading toward the surface, but sometimes the numbers seemed to indicate it was slowing down. Then the numbers would show it was rising again. Three endless hours after the crash, *Trieste* finally saw daylight. The gas balloon had held. Ballard had lived to dive another day. But he vowed it would never again be in a bathyscaph.

Apart from this close call, the Cayman Trough expeditions did much to deepen scientific knowledge of the earth's geology. But they failed to turn up something that Ballard and many other oceanographers were sure existed: deep-sea hot springs. Where plates were moving apart and cracks opening in the crust, they believed that seawater must be cycling down to be heated inside the earth before coming out again into the ice-cold bottom water. The most likely areas for such "hydrothermal vents" were places where the earth's plates are moving apart more rapidly than along the Mid-Atlantic Ridge. One of the most accessible of these faster-spreading centers is the Galápagos Rift, just northeast of the Galápagos Islands off the coast of Ecuador. And sure enough, previous surface expeditions in the area had recorded occasional slight rises in temperature in the rift valley. Were these temperature changes real, or had the instruments been wrong?

In February and March 1977, Ballard joined fifty scientists from all over the United States in an expedition to find and visit these vents. From the expedition leader down to the lowliest graduate student, every single person on the trip was a physical scientist—a geologist, geophysicist, or geochemist. Although life existed at these great depths, scientists believed that the deeper you went, the less life you would find. On this expedition, biologists wouldn't be needed.

Ballard had two main reasons for taking the trip—apart from his scientific curiosity about the vents themselves. For one thing, he had probably dived in submersibles more than anyone. For another, he knew how to operate ANGUS. Since ANGUS's debut during Project FAMOUS, the "dope on a rope" had gotten smarter. Its black-and-white still cameras had been replaced by color ones and the new Woods Hole research vessel, the *Knorr*, included facilities for developing the film on board. That meant that after each lowering, the scientists could find out exactly what ANGUS had seen.

The day before *Alvin* and the *Lulu* were due to arrive on site over the Galápagos Rift, the *Knorr* and ANGUS were already on the scene, searching for vents. For this expedition, ANGUS also carried a sensor that would register any change in temperature.

All night long, the *Knorr* towed the camera sled back and forth over a rough landscape more than eighty-five hundred feet below. Ballard's team at the surface was flying blind, using sonar to keep the sled no more than fifteen feet above the bottom and navigating by means of the usual network underwater transponder beacons. These are just like radio beacons, only they send out sound waves instead of radio waves. A computer on board ship instantly calculated the robot's exact position inside their transponder "net." However, even this system was not enough to prevent several crashes into rocky outcrops. But only once during that first twelve-hour lowering did the camera sled's sensors record any significant change in temperature.

With ANGUS back on board, its four-hundred-foot-long roll of film was unloaded and taken to the lab for processing while Ballard and his team grabbed a couple hours of sleep. Then they gathered to look at what ANGUS had seen, wondering what the brief temperature change could mean. At first they stared at frame after frame of bizarre pillow lava formations similar to those found during Project FAMOUS.

Then it happened. In one frame, nothing but lava.

The camera sled ANGUS (left) was towed over the Galápagos Rift, eighty-five hundred feet below the ocean's surface. Here Ballard and his team discovered an amazing colony of giant clams (below).

In the next, hundreds of white clams and brown mussels shimmered in a cloud of misty blue water. This unexpected undersea oasis lasted for just thirteen frames, only those pictures taken during the time ANGUS had also registered a tiny temperature change in the bottom water. After that the familiar lava landscape returned, virtually empty of life.

Ballard knew that ANGUS had discovered something special. How special only became evident in the days that followed. *Alvin's* first dive was to "Clambake I," as the ANGUS discovery soon became known. The three-man sub crew couldn't believe their eyes: The clams were huge, some as much as twelve inches across. How could they thrive so deep and so far from the light of the sun?

The first clue to this mystery came from the water samples *Alvin* brought back to the surface. As soon as they were opened in the shipboard lab, the sulfur stink of rotten eggs filled the air. The cause was hydrogen sulfide, a chemical compound created when seawater is heated inside the earth's crust. It was known that some bacteria could live off hydrogen sulfide. The same bacteria are found in garbage dumps and swamps. Was this the key to so much life so deep?

Soon the expedition found more hydrothermal vents, each one unique and several supporting truly amazing communities of undersea animals. The most remarkable of all, discovered on *Alvin's* eleventh dive, was immediately nicknamed the Garden of Eden. Here the shimmering deep-sea water was an incredible sixty-three degrees Fahrenheit. The standard water temperature at this depth is just above freezing. The variety of creatures was mind-boggling. *Alvin* found not only giant clams and mussels, but white crabs, pink fish with blue eyes, and most amazing of all, bright red worms living in white tubes up to eight feet long. Most of these creatures were completely new to science. As one of the scientists said at the time, "There was so much to learn. It was a discovery cruise. It was like Columbus."

Although Ballard and his colleagues weren't biologists, they had made one of the most important biological discoveries ever in the deep ocean. Frantically they stored specimens in everything from Tupperware containers to plastic bags for marine biologists back home to study. On subsequent expeditions, eager biologists revisited these vent communities, and discovered new ones, identifying still more new species. What fascinated them most of all was how these creatures could survive so far from the light of the sun.

Nowhere on Earth had scientists ever discovered a whole web of life that didn't depend on photosynthesis. Photosynthesis is the process by which green plants use sunlight to turn the carbon dioxide in the air into sugar. And sugar is the basic food of life. Normally food chains on land and in the water start with green plants. Some animals eat the plants. Others eat the plant eaters. And so on. That's how a food chain works. But how did this underwater food chain work? Without green plants, what was its first link?

Soon the biologists discovered the answer. The

communities that lived around the hydrothermal vents had replaced the energy of sunlight with energy from inside the earth. Their existence depended on a rare process called chemosynthesis.

In chemosynthesis, tiny bacteria that thrive in hydrogen sulfide take the place of green plants. The bacteria are able to use the earth's energy to combine hydrogen with carbon dioxide and produce sugar. This allows them to become the basis of the unique deep-ocean food chain found living at the hydrothermal vents. Some of the bacteria float in the water or cling to the surfaces and are eaten by the other vent species. It is a wonderful self-contained world without sun.

Two years later, in March 1979, Ballard's interest in the deep-sea hot springs led him to take part in an expedition to the East Pacific Rise, an area of the Mid-Ocean Ridge about two thousand miles north of the Galápagos Rift. Once again ANGUS made the first big discovery—a chimney belching what looked like black smoke but that was in fact superhot, mineral-rich water. This was a hydrothermal vent in the form of a deep-sea geyser. The temperature of these "black smokers" amazed Ballard and the other scientists who went down in *Alvin* for a closer look. When the sub's mechanical arm inserted a temperature probe into one of the chimneys, the gauge shot off the scale. Back on the surface, the team discovered that the glass tip of the probe had melted. Everyone suddenly realized that water that hot could have cracked *Alvin's* viewports. On the next visit, the pilots were

(Above) Scientists
discovered these giant
red worms in white
tubes living by deep-sea
hot springs.

(Left) Bob Ballard
takes a closer look at one
of the eight-foot worms.

careful to keep the submersible at a safe distance.

The hydrothermal vents and black smokers helped scientists solve a long-standing puzzle about seawater: Why does it remain at a constant level of saltiness instead of getting progressively saltier? Geochemists made their calculations and came up with the answer. Every ten million years or so all the seawater on Earth is recycled by passing through the earth's crust, where it is heated and absorbs some minerals while losing others. The constant chemistry of seawater is the result of this ongoing process.

As for chemosynthesis, it may hold out the possibility of life on other planets, even within our own solar system. Some scientists speculate that underground streams, even seas, may exist on apparently dead planets. If sulfide-rich vents exist in these deep oceans, then so too may a food chain similar to the ones found beneath the earth's oceans. Perhaps the first life on earth began around hot geysers at the bottom of the ancient sea.

Just thirty-seven years old, Bob Ballard had managed to take part in some of the most important discoveries ever made in underwater science. But he was restless. As he later told an interviewer, "In thirteen years I had managed to explore a mere forty miles of a forty-thousand-mile-long mountain range. Did I really want to spend the rest of my life exploring another eighty or one hundred at best?"

# CHAPTER 7

# *TITANIC* SCHEMES

NOW ROBERT BALLARD BEGAN TO THINK SERIOUSLY about going to look for the *Titanic*. It was unquestionably the most famous shipwreck of all time. When the brand-new ocean liner left the English port of Southampton on April 10, 1912, to begin its maiden voyage, it carried on board some of the wealthiest and most famous people of its time. It was, after all, the largest and most luxurious passenger ship ever built, with elegant dining rooms, lavish staterooms and opulent lounges—even a gymnasium—for its first-class passengers. These people wanted to be part of the *Titanic's* first Atlantic crossing, which they regarded as a major social event. They looked on the ship as a technological marvel in an age of marvels. This was a time when almost everyone believed in progress: Through the wonders of science the world would keep getting better and better. So strong was their faith in the ability of human beings to triumph over nature, that virtually every one of them thought the *Titanic* was "unsinkable," although its builders never actually made this claim.

For the first four days the voyage went splendidly. The sea was calm, the weather was good, and the passengers were delighted with the new ship. They strolled on the decks, read or wrote letters in the lounge, ate fancy meals in the dining saloon. Unknown to all except a few officers, however, the *Titanic's* radio room was receiving repeated warnings of icebergs and pack ice ahead. But the captain wasn't overly concerned. He had traveled this route many times before. So he altered course slightly, but kept barreling "full steam ahead." Perhaps he was overconfident. But he believed that the lookouts in the crow's nest high up in the foremast would spot an iceberg in good time for the *Titanic* to avoid it.

After sunset on April 14, the sea grew unnaturally calm and there was no moon to catch an iceberg in its ghostly gleam. A light mist hung over the water, making visibility even more difficult. Still the *Titanic* raced onward. The passengers who took a stroll on deck before turning in for the night noticed that the air temperature had dropped sharply, but they thought nothing of it. Soon all but a few stragglers playing cards in the first-class smoking room had gone to bed.

Just before 11:40 P.M., lookout Frederick Fleet squinted into the darkness—was there a shape out there? He did not have ship's binoculars so he was working at a handicap. The slight haze lying over the water added to his difficulties. But there was no

*(Above) When the Titanic left England on April 10, 1912, it was the world's largest and most luxurious liner. Inside the ship, passengers found elegant rooms and the Grand Staircase, (right) topped by a glass dome.*

question about it. A towering black object loomed directly in the huge ship's path. Quickly Fleet rang the bell three times, to warn the bridge, and picked up the telephone. "Iceberg right ahead," he told the officer at the other end. A great mountain of ice lay straight ahead and was closing fast.

The officers on the bridge scrambled to turn the ship, but there wasn't enough time. The starboard side of the *Titanic's* bow hit the berg with a sickening crunch and scraped along its side, damaging its hull plates. Water began pouring into the lower decks of the ship. Someone ran to find the captain. The unthinkable had happened.

Few of the passengers realized at first that anything was wrong. Some noticed a slight jar, but assumed it was nothing. But as the engines slowed, then stopped, and the ship drifted to a standstill, they realized something was surely amiss. Still, there could be no cause for alarm on this vast and solid vessel. Several of those who had been playing cards in the smoking room strolled out on deck to see what was going on. They came back carrying chunks of ice that had fallen from the berg as it passed. Most of the passengers treated the whole thing as a lark, a pleasant diversion in what had become a routine sea voyage.

But down in the engine rooms the story was very different. Below the waterline along the ship's starboard side, where the iceberg had scraped along the hull, the collision had sounded like a series of cannon shots. And now water was gushing into the ship, forcing the crews to scramble for safety. Most of the people on board didn't know it, but the "unsinkable" *Titanic* was sinking. Her so-called watertight compartments weren't watertight at all. They were open at the top. As one compartment filled, it overflowed into the next one. The mail room was already awash with floating bags of letters. The ship was doomed. It had one hour to live, maybe two.

After a quick tour below decks, the captain realized the worst. But he didn't sound the general alarm. He and his fellow officers knew a terrible fact about their wonderful new ship: It didn't have enough lifeboats. There were 2,200 people on board, but lifeboats for only 962. If this fact got out, there would be panic. So the captain instructed his officers to begin loading the lifeboats but not to say how serious the situation really was.

Many passengers were curious and came out on deck, but even when they saw the lifeboats being uncovered most still treated the whole thing as some kind of joke. The sea was flat calm and there was no sign of danger. An almost partylike atmosphere developed when the ship's band assembled in the lounge and began playing cheerful tunes.

Reluctantly a few people boarded the first boats, mostly women and children. Some wives refused to leave their husbands, and many of the early boats left the ship half empty. Gradually, however, as the ship's bow began to sink more noticeably, people crowded into the boats. At one point an officer had to brandish a revolver to prevent a stampede. Most of the first-class passengers got away safely, as did many of those in second class. But few of the third-class passengers, separated from the boat deck by locked doors and long passageways, even had a chance.

The slope of the deck grew steeper and steeper. Some people jumped into boats as they were being lowered. Others leapt into the icy water. But most clung to the ship. Soon hundreds of people were gathered on the stern as it rose higher and higher. Then with a great crash the stern settled back, almost as if the ship were righting itself. Moments later it disappeared from sight. It was 2:20 A.M. on April 15, 1912.

Those in the lifeboats listened in horror to the screams of the hundreds of people who were freezing to death in the cold water. But only one boat returned to rescue them. Most of those who were safe feared these desperate swimmers would overturn their boats and drown everyone. Gradually the last cries and moans faded away, and the lifeboats were left to drift on the silent, empty ocean. Did anyone know the *Titanic* had sunk? the survivors wondered. Would they be rescued?

In fact, the liner *Carpathia*, which had received the *Titanic*'s distress signal, was already dashing to the scene. Its captain threw caution overboard and charged at full speed, dodging icebergs with only the stars to light the way. Just as dawn was tinging the horizon, those in the lifeboats saw the *Carpathia*'s flares. By the time day had broken, the rescue ship was

*(Above) The sinking* Titanic *sent off signal flares in the hope that some nearby ship would come to its rescue. It was not until the next morning that the rescue ship* Carpathia *arrived to pluck the* Titanic's *few lifeboats (below) from the sea.*

taking on survivors. Some had clung all night to one overturned lifeboat; their feet and legs were numb with the cold and they were in danger of freezing to death. The *Carpathia's* captain couldn't believe his eyes. These few, sad lifeboats were all that remained of the mighty *Titanic*. Of its twenty-two hundred passengers, more than fifteen hundred had perished.

Since that terrible night, the *Titanic* has lived in the popular imagination through movies and books. Many people had talked of going to search for the wreck. Some had even talked about trying to raise it to the surface. The craziest of these schemes involved filling its hull with Ping Pong balls. Ballard knew that if he didn't organize an expedition soon someone else would beat him to the prize.

His first serious attempt came in the fall of 1977. The Director of the Woods Hole Oceanographic Institution gave Ballard permission to conduct a series of sea trials with a ship called the *Alcoa Seaprobe*, which Alcoa Aluminum was considering giving to WHOI. If the trials were successful, Ballard might get the green light to use the *Seaprobe* to go after the *Titanic*.

Early in October, the *Seaprobe* left Woods Hole with a team handpicked by Ballard and with a whole lot of borrowed equipment: a fancy side-scan sonar that could send sound waves out to both sides, providing a picture of a broad swath of the ocean floor (ideal for searching for a shipwreck); a deep-towed magnetometer that would detect even the smallest piece of the *Titanic's* iron hull, and an underwater camera system more advanced than ANGUS. The *Seaprobe* was far from ideal for Ballard's purposes. It resembled the vessels used in drilling undersea oil wells—with a tall metal derrick rising above the "moon pool," a big hole in the middle of the ship. Ballard's high-tech equipment had to be attached to a piece of pipe and then painstakingly lowered through the moon pool. Every sixty feet, a new piece of pipe had to be added, until the required depth was achieved. It made for a slow and laborious process. And unlike the towing equipment for ANGUS, which consisted of a long cable attached to a big winch drum on the deck, this system could not be quickly raised to avoid obstacles. Nonetheless Ballard hoped it would do the trick.

It took most of the first day to lower the vehicle pod carrying the borrowed sonar and the camera system to the planned test depth of three thousand feet—sixty feet above the bottom. Then most of the exhausted crew headed for their bunks while the ship began some test sonar runs. Ballard and a skeleton team kept the overnight watch, working in the control center overlooking the moon pool. By two in the morning, he was only half awake, listening vaguely to the pinging of the sonar and staring vacantly at the printout as the ship steamed slowly along its track.

Suddenly, a crash louder than thunder exploded over his head. As he leapt to his feet, he watched the top piece of the drill pipe disappear into the water. By the time he reached the edge of the moon pool, all that remained of his expensive equipment was the snapped-off communications cable, spitting sparks as it dangled from the derrick. It could have been worse. The derrick's huge counterweight had crashed onto the deck above the control center. Fortunately it hadn't punched its way through to the people working below.

Ballard stared in stunned silence at the cold, empty water, wondering what had gone wrong. He found out later that an inexperienced foreman had failed to install a special reinforced section of pipe to be used when towing heavy equipment. As a result, the unreinforced pipe had snapped. Insurance would pay for the lost high-tech gadgetry, but Ballard knew his dream had just gone up in smoke.

After this kind of setback, many people would have given up and gone on to other things. But Ballard wasn't prepared to abandon the *Titanic* just yet. Nor was his new friend Bill Tantum, president of the Titanic Historical Society. William H. Tantum IV, affectionately known as "Mr. Titanic," was the *Titanic* buff to end all *Titanic* buffs. His house was filled with *Titanic* memorabilia, and his mind seemed to contain every fact as well as every fantasy about the famous ocean liner. Through him, Ballard had learned to think of the ship as much more than a famous wreck lost in deep water. He had begun to relive the tragic story and to feel as if he personally knew many of the passengers and crew on board the doomed liner.

After the *Seaprobe* setback, Ballard, Tantum, and *National Geographic* photographer Emory Kristof formed a company to raise the money to back a *Titanic* expedition. They pitched their idea to everyone they could think of. In May 1978, it looked like Roy Disney Jr., whose father had taken over the Disney empire when his brother Walt died, was prepared to give them the go-ahead. But the cost and the risk finally scared him off. All the avenues they tried led to dead ends. Then, in 1980, Bill Tantum died. That same year someone else mounted an expedition to look for the *Titanic*. This was a Texas oil millionaire by the name of Jack Grimm.

No question, Grimm was a character. He had already bankrolled expeditions to look for Noah's Ark (on a mountain in Turkey), the Loch Ness monster (in northern Scotland), and the Abominable Snowman (in Tibet). He tried to persuade the scientists he had hired for his first *Titanic* expedition to take along a monkey named Titan, whom he had trained to point to the place on the map where the ship was reported to have sunk. They refused.

Grimm mounted three expeditions to look for the wreck of the *Titanic*. Only on the second one, in the summer of 1981, did he bring back any hint of a ship. This was a blurry photo mosaic of something he claimed was the *Titanic's* huge propeller. But when he returned to the propeller site the following year, there was no sign of either it or of a shipwreck. As Ballard watched Grimm's shenanigans, he began to believe that he would get another shot at making the historic discovery, after all.

By 1983 quite a few things had changed in Bob Ballard's life. His many scientific publications about his deep-sea geological researches had helped him climb the academic ladder at Woods Hole, where he was now a tenured senior scientist. And he had founded the Deep Submergence Laboratory (DSL) to develop and test pioneering technology for ocean research.

Ballard had long been dissatisfied with the oceanographic tools he had been using. There were some wonderful sonar gadgets and various camera vehicles more sophisticated than ANGUS. But a scientist who believed like Ballard that there was no substitute for the human eyeball at the bottom of the ocean still had to depend on submersibles like *Alvin* to take him down there. The trouble was, an *Alvin* dive could last no more than nine hours. The deeper the dive, the less time the sub could spend on the bottom. As a result, oceanographers spent far too much time commuting to and from work. There was also the ever-present danger of sending human beings deep into inner space. If a remotely operated vehicle got stuck all you lost was expensive equipment. If *Alvin* got stuck, you lost three people's lives. Furthermore, the working conditions in the cold, cramped sphere were awful— something Ballard knew as well as anyone.

For some time he'd been dreaming about a remotely controlled robot system that would be as good as or better than human eyes and human hands on the bottom and that could be operated twenty-four hours a day from a control room on a surface ship. He even had a name for his dream—*Argo/Jason*. Jason was the character in Greek mythology who set out in search of the golden fleece. The *Argo* was his ship. Argo and Jason seemed perfect names for robots that would search the ocean depths and make new scientific discoveries.

As early as 1981, Ballard described this dream for an article in *National Geographic*. He painted a romantic picture of his vision of a remote television system that would allow a scientist sitting comfortably in his or her command center on a ship at the surface to feel as if he or she were walking along the ocean floor. Ballard called this dream "telepresence." In many ways, he argued, it would be better than actually being there.

A fiber-optic cable would carry instant television images to the support ship, enabling the surface team to react fast to changing conditions on the bottom. No more crashing ANGUS into unseen submarine outcroppings. The scientists' "eyes" and "ears" would be the two robots named *Argo* and *Jason*. *Argo*, the larger of the two, mounted with multiple video cameras and sonars, would have a broad view of the bottom terrain. When *Argo* found something interesting, it would hover in place while *Jason* went off to investigate. This smaller, self-propelled robot, attached to *Argo* by a fiber-optic tether, would be able to venture into places not safe for the larger vehicle. Using its two video-camera lenses much like human eyes, it would gather samples with its mechanical arms. Finally, Ballard imagined this whole system linked to an earth-orbiting satellite that would permit instant transmission of what *Argo* and *Jason* were looking at to any satellite receiver anywhere in the world. Even a person thousands of miles away could feel like he or she was at the scene.

This grand conception was still only a gleam in Ballard's eye back in 1981. But in 1983, the team he'd assembled at the Deep Submergence Laboratory quickly began work on an *Argo* prototype. And soon, a two-ton, fifteen-foot long camera sled was taking shape in the basement workrooms at DSL, funded with money from Ballard's old friends at the Office of Naval Research.

He still dreamed of going to look for the *Titanic*. What had begun as a technological challenge, then developed into a growing fascination, had by now become an obsession. Grimm had failed. Now it was his turn. But how to raise the money?

The Navy's interest in *Argo* gave Ballard an idea. Early in 1984, he approached the Navy with a proposal for testing the *Argo* prototype. The test area? A grim stretch of the north Atlantic southeast of Newfoundland where the continental shelf plunges downward to meet the deep-ocean's abyssal plain. Perfect geography to show off *Argo*'s capabilities, he told them. And, oh, and by the way, we just might find the *Titanic* while we're at it.

To Ballard's delight, the Navy agreed to fund a three-week *Argo* trial for the summer of 1985. But

*Ballard dreamed of the day when humans would not have to risk their lives on deep-ocean dives. Instead, robots like* Argo *(above) and* Jason *(seen left, with* Argo*) would transmit images of what they had seen via surface ship and satellite anywhere in the world (left).*

given Grimm's failure, Ballard realized that three weeks probably wasn't enough time to be sure of finding the wreck. Then he thought of the many French friends he had made during Project FAMOUS and subsequent expeditions. He knew the French loved a technological challenge. Perhaps they would join forces with him and bring along their brand-new side-scan sonar, SAR.

Sure enough, the director of the French Ocean-ographic Institute, IFREMER, was as excited as Ballard about the prospect of going after the *Titanic*. Soon everything was set. The only challenge left was actually locating the wreck. That would prove more difficult than anyone imagined.

# CHAPTER 8

# THE GREATEST DISCOVERY

NEAR THE BEGINNING OF JULY 1985, THE FRENCH research ship *Le Suroit* arrived near the place where the *Titanic* had sunk a little over seventy-three years before. In command was Ballard's old friend Jean-Louis Michel of IFREMER, who had designed and built SAR. They both believed that this state-of-the-art deep-towed sonar was just the piece of technology to find the wreck. For the next two weeks, *Le Suroit* patiently "mowed the lawn," towing SAR back and forth along one thousand-meter-wide tracks within the designated search area, "like a kite on a two-and-half-mile string," Ballard later wrote. When Ballard arrived on board *Le Suroit* two weeks later, on July 22, he found his friend tired and discouraged. SAR had given Michel a lovely portrait of the ocean floor, but found not the slightest trace of *Titanic* wreckage.

Not for the first time, Ballard wondered if they were looking in the right place. The only things known for sure about the *Titanic*'s sinking position were the coordinates radioed from the ship when it sent out its distress call. But these were based on what is known as dead reckoning. Just before sunset on April 14, 1912, one of the ship's officers had taken a sighting of the sun and certain stars. This process, known as celestial navigation, was then the most accurate way of fixing a ship's position. However, by the time the *Titanic* hit the iceberg the ship had been traveling for many hours. Its actual sinking position was calculated by estimating the distance traveled since the celestial fix at sunset. This is dead reckoning, obviously an inaccurate process, especially since a current can greatly affect the distance a ship can cover. The actual wreck could be miles from where the distress signal said it was.

In sifting all the clues, Ballard and Michel had come down to two fundamental conclusions. One was that the *Titanic*'s dead reckoning position was too far west since it put the ship in the middle of an icefield it was steaming toward but never reached. How far east it might really have been was suggested by the position of the lifeboats when the *Carpathia* found them the following morning—more than ten miles southeast of the official position. It was known that another ship that had stopped for the night nearby had drifted a little over five miles south in the current. So the lifeboats must have drifted that way, too. The wreck of the *Titanic* ought to be east of the official position and north of the lifeboats. At least, that's what Ballard and Michel figured. Accordingly they had drawn a square target area within which they would focus their search. The *Titanic*'s stated sinking position was at the western boundary of this square and the lifeboat recovery position near the southern boundary. The wreck had to be inside this square—they hoped.

Two weeks later, on August 6, after a full month of fruitless searching with SAR, Ballard and Michel wondered if any of their assumptions were correct. *Le Suroit*'s time was up and still not even a whisper of wreckage had appeared on SAR's high-resolution sonar printout. They had searched seventy percent of the target area. Perhaps the wreck was hidden in some submarine canyon or buried beneath a mudslide. Perhaps it was lost forever.

Less than two weeks remained in what had at first seemed an ample six-week expedition. The original plan had been for *Le Suroit* to find the wreck—a piece of cake—then ANGUS and *Argo* would explore it, taking both still pictures and video footage. Now Ballard and Michel were forced to improvise. As they returned to the search site aboard Woods Hole's *Knorr*, they plotted a desperation strategy: Use *Argo* to find the wreck.

Ballard's idea was simple. If, as he believed, the current that night flowed north to south, so must have the *Titanic*'s wreckage as it sank to the bottom. No ship sinks to the bottom in a single piece; instead it leaves a trail of debris behind it. The stronger the current and the deeper the wreck, the longer this "debris trail." Instead of looking for the wreck, they would look for the debris, running *Argo* in a series of east-west lines at right angles to the expected trail. Based on a current of 0.7 knots and a sinking depth of two and half miles, they calculated that the *Titanic's* telltale trail should be close to a mile long. Since SAR had already covered most of the old target area, they expanded their target square to the east. As extra insurance, each *Argo* run would overlap the previous SAR coverage.

Apart from a few technical glitches, *Argo* performed superbly. But as the days wore on, its video cameras revealed nothing but a mind-numbing landscape of mud, mud, and more mud. A major event was the sight of a holothurian, a bottom-dwelling creature that looks like a huge slug. The round-the-clock watch schedule—four hours on, four hours off—was wearing everyone down. Morale dropped and there were growing grumblings that the whole exercise was a waste of time.

Spirits hit rock bottom on August 31, only five days before *Knorr* was due to head home. The weather was getting steadily worse and most of the expanded search area had now been covered by *Argo*. There were only a few lines left to run. Ballard and Michel stared failure in the face.

That evening after supper, Ballard stayed in the control van until midnight, staring glumly at the endless black and white *Argo* video of bottom mud. Finally, he had had enough and headed for his cabin. But he found he couldn't sleep. So he picked up a copy of the book he'd been reading, the life story of Chuck Yeager, the famous pilot. In the late forties when Ballard's dad had worked briefly in the Mojave Desert as a test flight engineer, he had known Yeager. A few years later Yeager was the first man to fly faster than the speed of sound.

Shortly after one in the morning, Ballard was still engrossed in Yeager's story when the ship's cook stuck his head inside the cabin door. "The guys think you should come down to the van," he said. In an instant, the book and breaking the sound barrier were forgotten. Ballard pulled on a jumpsuit over his pajamas and charged past the cook, almost flying down the three decks to the control van. Inside the room, crowded with instruments, video screens, and computer readouts, the atmosphere was electric.

"We've just passed over a boiler," one of the watch team announced excitedly. No one dared to declare that the boiler belonged to the *Titanic*. Ballard frantically reversed the *Argo* video to 1:13 A.M., only a few minutes earlier. As the tape replayed he watched a massive round shape pass before his eyes. He didn't need to look at the reference books. He had seen pictures of the *Titanic's* boilers a thousand times. This was it. The long hunt was over. He turned to shake Jean-Louis Michel's hand.

Around him the watch team erupted in war whoops and shouts of joy as the magnitude of that small video image sank in. Soon word spread, and it seemed that everyone on the ship had crowded into the van. Larger and larger chunks of wreckage now appeared—twisted hull plating, portholes, a piece of railing turned on its side. Ballard suddenly realized *Argo* was in danger of getting caught in the wreck's rigging and ordered the sled pulled up to a safer altitude. Then someone broke out the wine being saved for just this occasion. It looked like people were ready to party all night.

Until, that is, someone glanced at the clock. It was almost 2 A.M., local time, uncannily close to the hour the *Titanic* had sunk. As quickly as spirits had soared, they crashed to the bottom as the human meaning of those fragments of wreckage hit home.

"I don't know how you people feel," Ballard said, "but in about twenty minutes I'm going out on the fantail. If anyone wants to join me, they're welcome."

In ones and twos people drifted from the van. But a large crowd showed up twenty minutes later on the *Knorr's* fantail, the broad stern deck where *Argo* was launched and recovered. There Ballard led a brief memorial service for the men, women, and children who died when the *Titanic* went down. Ballard later wrote, "It was one thing to have won—to have found the ship. It was another thing to be there. That was the spooky part. I could see the *Titanic* as she slipped nose first into the glassy water. Around me were the ghostly shapes of the lifeboats and the piercing shouts and screams of people freezing to death in the water."

After a few moments of silence, the crowd on the fantail went back to their cabins, alone with their

*(Above) Bob Ballard (right) and French partner Jean-Louis Michel (center) plot their strategy for finding the* Titanic. *(Below) After weeks of searching, the team celebrates finding the wreck.*

thoughts. The next day they would all be looking at the wreck of the *Titanic* for the first time.

In the few days remaining, *Argo* and ANGUS took the historic pictures of the *Titanic* wreck that would soon appear on television screens and in magazines around the world. The huge passenger ship had broken into two main pieces. A section of the bow about 450 feet long sat upright in the bottom mud, looking very much as it had when the ship left the surface. Almost a third of a mile away lay what remained of the stern, a mangled wasteland of twisted metal surrounded by a field of devastation. It seemed the ship had broken in two at or near the surface, spilling its innards as it fell. When they plotted the wreck's position they found that *Le Suroit* had narrowly missed the *Titanic* during its very first sonar run, when the ship had been pushed off course by high winds and heavy seas.

The stage was now set for what would become *Alvin*'s most celebrated dive of all, far eclipsing its recovery of the hydrogen bomb off Spain, its descent to the Mid-Atlantic Ridge in 1974, or to the hydrothermal vents and black smokers in 1977 and 1979. Bob Ballard was about to see his dream come true. He was going to take a personal tour of the world's most famous shipwreck.

The discovery of the *Titanic* changed Bob Ballard's life for good. No longer was he the upstart young scientist who often rubbed his older colleagues the wrong way because of his ability to popularize his work. Suddenly he was a famous explorer, a guest on talk shows, courted by publishers to tell his story. His showman instincts came to the fore and he reveled in the limelight and the attention. Some grumbled that he took too much credit for the *Titanic* discovery, which was unquestionably a group effort. However, he was painstaking in giving credit to the French and particularly to the expedition coleader, Jean-Louis Michel. But Ballard was the star the media loved. And he seemed to love the role. It often appeared as if he and he alone had found the ship.

His wife and sons found Ballard's fame less easy to take—especially when reporters and television cameras camped outside their Cape Cod house demanding interviews. The police had to be called in to tame the media monster. Having a famous father put extra pressure on Todd and Douglas, now both in high school—particularly Todd. Ironically, he seems to have felt the same sort of inadequacy his father felt as a teenager, when Ballard competed with a father and a brother he believed were smarter and more accomplished than he could ever be. But whether Todd liked it or not, his father would never again be a relatively obscure scientist. From now on he would be the man who found the *Titanic*.

The summer after the discovery, in July 1986, Ballard led a second expedition to the *Titanic* wreck. Once again the Navy was helping pay the bill—this time because Ballard would be testing *Jason Junior*, an early version of *Jason*. *JJ*, as the robot soon came to be called, was mounted in a garage attached to the front of *Alvin* and could be "driven" from a set of controls inside the sub. Its 250-foot tether would allow *JJ* to go where *Alvin* couldn't—inside the hull of the sunken ship. With its single video camera it immediately earned the nickname, "the swimming eyeball."

The first dive to the wreck, on July 13, proved unlucky. Ballard caught only a brief glimpse of the steel wall of the bow rising up into the darkness, before battery problems forced *Alvin* to return to the surface. The next day, however, the two-and-a-half hour descent went smoothly, and *Alvin* landed close to the *Titanic*'s forward section. As the sub approached the ship, the knife-edge of the bow suddenly appeared right in front of them. Instinctively, Ballard pulled back. He'd reacted as if the ship was in motion, about to run him down!

The pilot brought the sub gently up along the port side, past the giant anchor, then along the line of portholes whose glass was still unbroken, but which wept huge icicles of rust. These were soon dubbed "rusticles." Then they rose up and over the metal railing until they were floating a few feet above the forward deck. A great bronze-topped capstan and the two huge anchor chains were still attached to their winches. But the wooden decking was gone! It turned out that wood-boring molluscs had eaten it away. Finally, with everyone in the sub holding his breath, *Alvin* landed with a gentle clank on the metal subdeck just forward of the main mast. The deck held. They would be able to make other landings.

*Alvin* rose up again and headed toward the bridge. The mast, with the crow's nest still visible, had fallen aft across the well deck. The current was strong and the pilot was worried, but Ballard wasn't. He was having the time of his life. "We're fine," he said. "The bridge should be dead ahead. Come right."

There it was. The wooden wheelhouse was gone, but the ship's bronze telemotor control, where the wheel was once attached, stood in the spot where the quartermaster had desperately spun it in a vain attempt to avoid the iceberg. The golden metal gleamed in *Alvin*'s lights, polished to a sheen by the underwater currents. They landed briefly to test the deck strength—again no problem—then moved on, past the gaping hole where the number-one funnel had been, until they were hovering over the opening where once an elegant glass dome had shed natural light on the *Titanic*'s first-class Grand Staircase. But *JJ*'s motors had flooded and weren't working. Its "walk" into the ship's interior would have to wait for another day.

*Alvin* now headed west, toward the port side and dropped down to peer in the windows of the A-Deck promenade. It was here that many of the wealthiest passengers boarded lifeboats, husbands saying good-bye to their wives and children for the last time.

The hull of the ship now acted as a buffer against the deep-sea current and *Alvin* easily held its position

*The* Titanic's *stern section (above) lies 1,970 feet away from the bow section. In* Alvin, *Ballard (right) explored the debris field around the wreck and photographed objects that had fallen from the ship as it sank, such as this metal footboard from a bed (below).*

On the forward deck of the bow section *(above)*, Jason Junior *(below)* examined the huge bollards around which ropes had been tied when the ship was in dock. JJ found the bronze telemotor control to which the ship's wooden wheel was once attached *(left)* on the bridge.

as Ballard peered into the covered walkway. *Alvin's* lights reflected eerily off the interior windows. Ballard later wrote about this moment: "Here I was on the bottom of the ocean peering at recognizable, man-made artifacts designed and built for another world. I was looking through windows out of which people had once looked, at decks along which they had walked, into rooms where they had slept and joked and made love. It was like landing on the surface of Mars only to find the remains of an ancient civilization similar to our own—a live episode from *The Twilight Zone.*"

As the pilot lifted *Alvin* up toward the boat deck, the sub shuddered suddenly and there was a loud clanging noise. A shower of rust particles fell past Ballard's viewport. No one panicked, but all three men knew that an unseen overhang could be big trouble. The pilot backed carefully away from the hull, hoping nothing had snagged the little sub. So far so good. Then he rose up slowly. There was the culprit—a lifeboat davit that had fallen over, projecting several feet out from the side. Its block still dangled from the end. All Ballard could think of was the tragedy of too few lifeboats. Too many lives lost.

Another battery problem forced an early end to Ballard's first tour of the *Titanic*. But it was not his last. Each visit increased his knowledge of the ship—its splendor and the awful devastation. Finally, several days later, *Alvin* finally landed on the *Titanic's* deck next to the Grand Staircase opening. One of *JJ*'s designers, Martin Bowen, sat with the *JJ* control box in his lap as the pint-sized robot emerged for the first time from its garage and headed into the unknown. Bowen knew any slip on his part meant this priceless piece of equipment might be lost. If the robot became tangled, its tether would be cut so that *Alvin* could escape.

Ever so slowly, Bowen inched *JJ* out of its garage and toward the opening, using its four small motors to turn it into a Hovercraft underwater. The joystick in his right hand controlled direction. The pistol grip in his left controlled *JJ*'s altitude. It was like playing a sophisticated computer game. He began to drop *JJ* down, down, until it disappeared from their viewports. All three men stared at the video monitor inside the sub—*JJ* was now their eyes. The wooden stairway itself was gone, with no sign of its ornate oak and iron railings or the statue of a cherub holding a lamp in the form of a flame. Perhaps all traces of its former grandeur had vanished. But no. Blurrily in the distance through a doorway at the A deck level, a faint, dangling object appeared. *JJ* moved closer and the vague shape slowly turned into an intact light fixture, still hanging from its wire but with a feathery sea-pen jutting jauntily from it.

As *JJ* swam into the room, its tether brushed against some rusticles hanging from the ceiling and the little ROV was suddenly lost in an orange cloud. But Bowen didn't panic. Soon the cloud cleared and he guided the robot to within a foot of the "chandelier," snapping wonderful still pictures as well as video footage. Then, with the same painstaking care, Bowen guided *JJ* back to its garage in front of *Alvin*. When the submarine returned to the surface Ballard and Bowen felt like conquering heroes. *JJ* had performed like a veteran. Through its video eyeball, they had peered inside the *Titanic*.

In all, Ballard made nine dives to the *Titanic* wreck site and debris field. *Alvin* landed on the boat deck and on the blasted stern, leaving a memorial plaque to Ballard's friend Bill Tantum, who had helped keep his *Titanic* dream alive, and to all those who died when the ship went down. On that same dive, *Alvin* drove in under the stern until it was almost touching the ship's huge rudder, but didn't find a propeller. A later expedition did, which only proves how difficult working in tiny subs and poor visibility can be. *JJ* peered inside portholes and through the windows of several first-class cabins. It found a metal sign that read, THIS DOOR FOR CREW USE ONLY.

Some of the most fascinating discoveries turned up in the debris field. When the *Titanic* broke in two at the surface, an incredible rain of artifacts spilled out from its insides. These were now scattered in a huge area around the stern. *Alvin* came across a White Star Line teacup—the red flag insignia still visible—sitting on a boiler as if placed there only moments ago. There were many poignant reminders of the human activity that had ceased so suddenly when the ship sank: a copper sink and several pots and pans from the kitchen; a washbasin from one of the staterooms; a

*(Above)* Alvin *waits on the deck as* Jason Junior *explores the ruined Grand Staircase. It was here that* JJ *found this intact light fixture (top right). Scattered around the wreck were objects like this bathtub (bottom right), sad reminders of the life once lived on the* Titanic.

champagne bottle with the cork still in it; a hairbrush, a hand mirror, and a pair of shoes. Most moving of all was a doll's head lying bald and unloved on the ocean floor. Once it had belonged to one of the many children who traveled on the *Titanic's* maiden voyage.

Among the most tantalizing objects discovered in the debris field was one of the ship's safes. When *Alvin's* arm attempted to open the safe, however, it proved to have no back. But even had it contained gold or valuable jewelry, Ballard would have left it on the bottom. He had already sworn to leave the wreck as he found it. After all, it was the graveyard for more than fifteen hundred people.

Ballard's book about the discovery and exploration of the *Titanic* sold a million copies in eight languages and helped make his name familiar in places he'd never even visited. He was in demand as a lecturer, packing halls all over North America as he recreated his greatest adventure before rapt audiences. But even as he savored the fame and fortune his *Titanic* success had brought him, his thoughts turned toward fresh challenges.

## CHAPTER 9

# NEW FRONTIERS

IN THE EARLY PART OF MAY 1989, BOB BALLARD'S DREAM of telepresence—bringing distant television viewers in on the act of discovery—became a reality. In special video theaters across a network of museums in Canada and the United States, two hundred thousand elementary school students watched as the brand-new *Jason* robot hovered over the remains of an ancient Roman shipwreck. Martin Bowen, the man who drove *Jason Junior* down the *Titanic*'s Grand Staircase, was once again at the controls, but this time he sat comfortably in a gadget-filled control van on board a ship called the *Star Hercules*, floating almost three thousand feet above the wreck off the western tip of Sicily. With practiced skill, Martin moved *Jason* toward its target, a large North African cargo jar called an amphora that had been lost in a shipwreck during the fourth century A.D. He then buried *Jason*'s specially designed scoop in the sediment beneath the jar. Finally, with a satisfying plop, the amphora settled into the net. Then the robot carried the jar to an underwater elevator. Once full, the elevator dropped its weights and rose to the surface with its load of treasure from the past.

For the next week, as *Jason* continued exploring the shipwreck—nicknamed *Isis* after the ancient patron goddess of sailors—Ballard and his team of experts broadcast six one-hour shows a day, each one for a different set of museum audiences many thousands of miles away. Each show was different, reflecting the marine archaeology going on as the broadcast was taking place. This was science in action.

The *Isis* broadcasts were part of Ballard's newest enterprise, the JASON Project. They combined his passion for the development of new deep-sea technology and his newfound fascination with underwater archaeology. But above all they were about getting young people excited about science. It was Ballard's belief that the marvel of telepresence could rekindle interest in scientific disciplines, an area where North Americans had begun to lag far behind other developed countries. To this end he had raised the money and founded an educational foundation that would mount one major two-week-long expedition to a different ocean location each year.

The idea soon took off. The next year, *Jason* explored the wrecks of two ships sunk in Lake Ontario during the War of 1812. For the first time students tuning in from the JASON sites were able to take the controls and drive the robot—just as if they were on board Ballard's ship. Then, Ballard and his team broadcast from the Galápagos Islands, where Charles Darwin gathered much of the evidence for his theory of evolution. And in the spring of 1993, *Jason* explored areas off Baja California, including active hydrothermal vents and deep-sea oases of life. Those 1993 shows reached more than seven hundred thousand students gathered at twenty-eight Primary Interactive Network sites, including new locations in Great Britain and Bermuda. But in May 1989, all this was still in the future. As the *Star Hercules* left the *Isis* wreck and headed toward its home port in Britain, a second and very different challenge occupied Ballard's mind: finding the wreck of the *Bismarck*, the powerful German battleship that was cornered and sunk on May 27, 1941, after a desperate chase involving almost all the ships in the British Navy. The previous summer, Ballard had searched for but failed to find the lost battleship despite the fact that its position was much more closely known than the *Titanic*'s. The *Bismarck* went down in broad daylight, with enemy ships all around, in the Atlantic ocean about six hundred miles west of Brest, France. But Ballard knew as well as anyone that finding a shipwreck is never easy. He has described it as being "like looking for a needle in a haystack in the middle of the night with a flashlight."

In this case the "flashlight" was once again *Argo*, whose success in locating the *Titanic* had convinced Ballard it was as good as any sonar at looking for lost wrecks. And Ballard's son Todd, now twenty, was one of the three *Argo* flyers on board. Ballard was extremely proud of how skilled his son had become at operating the *Argo* controls and of how he'd matured into a responsible member of the team since the previous year. On the 1988 expedition, Todd had been a real embarrassment, often sleeping past the beginning of his watch and behaving unreliably.

Once the *Star Hercules* reached the search area, Ballard and his team spent another frustrating week of the familiar routine of mowing the lawn. The two-hundred-square-mile search area was rapidly shrinking, yet not a single fragment of the *Bismarck*'s wreckage had passed before *Argo*'s video eyes. Maybe the battleship had exploded as it sank, leaving nothing to find.

As with the *Titanic*, Ballard missed the first moment of discovery. The evening of June 5, 1989, he was in the *Star Hercules* mess, playing a game of Trivial Pursuit with several other members of the team. But when his old friend, Woods Hole geologist Al Uchupi, walked in and announced matter-of-factly, "Bob, we've encountered some debris I think you should look at," Ballard catapulted out of his seat. He knew that Al would have been matter-of-fact even if there was an iceberg dead ahead.

This time no easily identifiable object like a ship's boiler swam into view. But Ballard and the crew in the control van watched with growing excitement as larger pieces of wreckage appeared. Then the debris field— if that's what it was—stopped cold. When they picked up the trail again, and tried to follow it, it led them to a dead end. The ship wasn't where it should have been.

The clues were confusing, but there was evidence of a huge underwater landslide. Had this buried the wreck? As the search continued, the clues accumulated. *Argo* found a number of larger pieces of wreckage—but nothing definitely from the *Bismarck*. About half a day after the first discovery they came across a chilling sight, a field of boots scattered on the bottom sediment, including one pair sitting side by side as if someone had just stepped out of them. Had these belonged to a German sailor? Finally, almost a full day after finding the first fragment of wreckage, a massive circular shape materialized beneath *Argo*'s video lens. "Bingo!" shouted someone in the van. There was no doubt this came from the German battleship. What they were looking at was the bottom of one of the *Bismarck*'s four giant gun turrets. But still the main wreck eluded them.

Yet another day passed, and another night. Just after 9 A.M. on the morning of June 8, Ballard was lying in his cabin after a too-brief sleep, staring idly at the video screens. (For this expedition he'd had a set of monitors installed in his sleeping quarters so he could watch with *Argo*'s eyes even when he wasn't in the van.) As he stared at the screen, a dim gray-white outcrop loomed in *Argo*'s forward-looking camera. This was nothing new. The avalanche had churned the bottom into all sorts of hills and valleys. *Argo* rose up to avoid the obstacle, then Ballard's jaw dropped. He was looking at two gun barrels jutting from a turret. That was no outcrop. That was the *Bismarck*.

The main wreck had been difficult to pinpoint

because of the way the avalanche had jumbled the evidence. When the hull had crashed into the bottom its weight had triggered the landslide, which had then carried the ship along with it. For the next several hours lighter debris, which falls more slowly, had rained down on this dramatically changed landscape. That was why the debris trail appeared to lead nowhere.

Once again Ballard's luck had held. Once again he returned to shore a conquering hero, this time with dramatic still and video pictures of an amazingly intact battleship with a German swastika dimly visible on its stern deck and dangerous-looking guns raised as if ready to fire. But fate was about to deal him a very unlucky card.

About a month after Ballard returned home to Cape Cod, his son Todd and a buddy were out late one night in the family Thunderbird. Todd was driving too fast, the car missed a turn, careened off the road, and smashed into a tree. Both boys died instantly. The tragedy devastated Ballard, his wife, Marjorie, and son Douglas. One moment Todd was there, the next he was gone. It seemed so senseless.

Only a few days earlier Todd had been with Ballard at a crowded press conference at National Geographic Headquarters in Washington, D.C. There his son watched proudly as he told the world about his discovery of the *Bismarck* and showed the first photographs of the wreck. Ballard had been in his element, at the top of his world. Now he had hit the depths.

He went through Todd's funeral in a state of shock.

*(Above)* Argo *shines its lights on the wreck of the battleship* Bismarck. *Its once-deadly antiaircraft guns are now decorated with sea anemones (right).*

125

But when he listened to the eulogy, delivered by one of the team members aboard the *Star Hercules*, the words must have penetrated deep. The eulogist had seen Todd grow from a boy into a man in a very short time. "Todd's fight to get there must have been tougher than most," he said. "Measuring up to friends, peers, parents, and siblings is no easy feat. But he had jumped out from behind these shadows and was beginning to cast his own." The same words could have been spoken about Ballard when he was Todd's age.

Ballard had experienced setbacks and disappointments in his life, rejections and failures, but nothing had prepared him for the loss of his elder son. The only way he knew how to cope with the tragedy was to stay in motion, planning the next JASON expedition, trying to raise money for another shipwreck hunt, putting the finishing touches on a novel he was co-authoring about a dashing underwater explorer. But the customary spark and sparkle were gone. He was going through the motions.

Time heals however. And Ballard has never been one to dwell on his misfortunes or to feel sorry for himself. He sought to turn Todd's death into something positive. If life could be snatched away so suddenly, all the more reason to make the most of the rest of his.

Not long after Todd's death, Ballard and Marjorie decided to end their marriage of twenty-four years. Their son Douglas was now at college and their lives had grown in different directions. In January 1991, Ballard married again. His bride was Barbara Earle,

Director of Development and Special Projects for National Geographic Television. Barbara quickly became his partner in more ways than one. She organized Ballard's next major expedition, to search for warships sunk off the South Pacific island of Guadalcanal, and participated as a full-fledged member of the expedition team.

Guadalcanal was unlike Ballard's previous hunts for sunken wrecks. This time he was looking for a whole fleet of Japanese, American, and Australian ships that had sunk over a six-month period in the second half of 1942. He would be exploring not a single wreck, but an entire battlefield—and a part of American history he felt close to. As a young boy growing up in San Diego in the late forties, he'd heard many stories of the bloody battles of the Pacific campaign of World War II. Now he was about to revisit the first and probably the most important of these contests. It had begun on August 7, 1942, when American Marines invaded the small and isolated island of Guadalcanal, hundreds of miles east of New Guinea. Their objective was an almost-completed Japanese airstrip that would soon threaten the American supply route to Australia. For the next six months the two sides fought desperately to gain control of the island. Finally the Americans had won. But not before they lost many ships and many men.

Ballard's goal was to find ships from each of the two major naval battles fought in or near the body of water that came to be known as Iron Bottom Sound because so many ships sank there. In the first, the Battle of Savo Island, a Japanese raiding force stole into Iron Bottom Sound after midnight and surprised the American invasion fleet, sinking four heavy cruisers without losing any ships themselves. It was one of the worst naval defeats in American history. The second major battle, known as the Naval Battle of Guadalcanal, was fought during early November when the struggle for the island could still have gone either way. The Japanese won the first round, a bloody and chaotic night brawl where two American admirals died. But the second and more decisive round went to the Americans, thanks to the big guns of two new battleships, the *South Dakota* and the *Washington*.

The biggest challenge for Ballard was not to find wrecks—nearly fifty ships had sunk in Guadalcanal waters—but to find suitable representatives of each phase of these two major battles. As usual, he pulled it off. In the end he located and identified thirteen ships, including the Australian heavy cruiser *Canberra*, the American heavy cruiser *Quincy*, and the Japanese battleship *Kirishima*. The wrecks were in every imaginable state—bows blown off, superstructures in ruins or completely gone, hulls twisted as if by a giant's grip. The saddest of all was the *Kirishima*. It had turned over as it sank and lay face down in the bottom mud with its huge rudders and propellers jutting helplessly upward.

Because the summer of 1992 was the fiftieth anniversary of the Guadalcanal invasion, the U.S. Navy decided to back Ballard's expedition in a big

*(Above) Bob Ballard discusses his work with young people aboard the research ship* Star Hercules *as part of his JASON Project activities. (Right) The submersible* Sea Cliff *(on right) and camera vehicle* Scorpio *(on left) explore the U.S destroyer* Monssen, *sunk at Guadalcanal.*

way. They lent him the submersible *Sea Cliff*, and a remotely-operated camera vehicle called *Scorpio*, which was a close cousin of *Jason*. The idea was for *Scorpio's* powerful lights to enhance *Sea Cliff*'s camera work. One of the main problems with submarine photography is "backscatter." This happens when sediment in the water bounces light back at its source in the same way a car's headlights reflect off fog.

Working over sunken wrecks is always risky—far riskier than deep-sea biological and geological studies. The ever-present danger of getting snagged by a cable or hooked on a piece of collapsing wreckage hangs over every dive. So far Ballard had been remarkably lucky in his career. Probably his worst moment in *Alvin* had been when the sub got temporarily hung up on one of the *Titanic's* lifeboat davits. However, working around all these different and very damaged wrecks Ballard knew that the odds were stacked against him.

Ballard's luck held until he was diving in *Sea Cliff* on the wreck of the H.M.A.S. *Canberra*, the powerful Australian heavy cruiser that had sunk soon after the Battle of Savo Island. The Navy pilot set the sub down too firmly near the *Canberra's* heavy anchor chain, which lay splayed across the bottom—too near for Ballard's liking. When the mud stirred up by the awkward landing had subsided, the pilot pumped out some ballast and attempted to lift off. The sub didn't move. In desperation, the pilot dropped all the auxiliary weights. The sub lifted a few feet—then stopped.

Ballard began to think that somehow *Sea Cliff* had gotten snagged by one of the anchor chains. "I thought I was going to die," he later said. Unlike *Alvin*'s, *Sea Cliff*'s personnel sphere could not be released from the hull in an emergency. If they were stuck, they were stuck.

The pilot requested that the surface ship send *Scorpio* to look at the sub's stern to see what was causing the problem. *Scorpio* could see nothing. The tension inside *Sea Cliff* rose. Then, slowly and inexplicably the sub broke free of the mud and lifted up beside the wreck.

There had been no snagging after all. The pilot had simply picked up so much bottom mud that it had acted like a huge additional weight. Although the alarm had been a false one, it reinforced Ballard's belief that it was crazy for people to explore shipwrecks in submarines—especially now that the *Argo/Jason* system had been perfected.

The Guadalcanal expedition took place soon after Bob Ballard's fiftieth birthday, a time when many people are beginning to think about their retirement. But his calendar was fuller than ever. His commitment to the JASON Foundation for Education meant each year he would mount another expedition and host live broadcasts to sites around the world. His fascination with famous shipwrecks would continue. In the summer of 1993, he and his wife, Barbara, led an expedition to explore the wreck of the *Lusitania*, sunk off the coast of Ireland by a torpedo from a German

U-boat on May 7, 1915. He was planning to write a book about the process and philosophy of discovery and to coauthor a second novel. Steven Spielberg had hired him as the scientific consultant for *Seaquest,* a science-fiction adventure series set in a submarine in the year 2017. (The character of the sub's commander was based on Ballard's.)

But all this activity wasn't enough. He was looking for another Mount Everest to climb—and not necessarily an underwater one. As far as Ballard is concerned, the great oceanographic discoveries of this century have been made. The greatest challenge now is to save the planet from humankind's own success. Ironically, for someone who reveres technology, he is increasingly determined to lend his name and prestige to the fight against the ravages that technology has wrought: pollution, poverty, overpopulation. He has long been one of those who regard the planet as a single living organism—Gaia. That organism is sick, he argues. Its lifeblood, the oceans and the atmosphere, is increasingly poisoned. Strong action is needed—before it's too late.

This has been the story of a life very much still in progress. No one can predict where Bob Ballard will go next. One thing seems sure, however. The questing energy that saw him through his darkest hours and helped him rise above his peers will take him on to new discoveries.

# EPILOGUE

## February 7, 1992

THE HIGH SCHOOL STUDENTS SHUFFLE RESTLESSLY IN their auditorium chairs as the school principal launches into a lengthy introduction of the guest speaker, a famous American scientist. They would rather be almost anywhere than listening to this boring list of the guest's accomplishments going back to his high school days. Then a vigorous, six-foot-two man strides confidently to the podium and, with hardly a pause, begins to speak. Despite the balding forehead, he looks younger than his fifty years. His voice is energetic, upbeat. His first joke gets a hearty round of laughter.

At first the room doesn't completely quiet down. But when the speaker describes landing his submarine on the *Titanic*'s deck, there is silence. When he flashes a picture on the screen of himself examining a giant tube worm on board a ship near the Galápagos Rift, there is a loud expression of disgust from the audience.

And when he talks about what it means to be an explorer, everybody seems to be listening.

Bob Ballard has given hundreds of speeches to adult and young audiences since the discovery that made him so well known. In the last few years, many of these talks have been part of his self-proclaimed mission to get young people interested in science, to inspire a generation of young explorers.

"I've spent my whole life dreaming up things and then going out and doing them," he tells his listeners. "I try to translate my dreams into reality." Ballard's message is incurably optimistic. "I view life as an epic journey," he continues. "An epic journey is never complete until you bring back the new truth that you've discovered and share it with others."

Looking back over Ballard's life you could argue that he gets his optimism from his upbringing, from those early and constant messages that he was meant to do something worthwhile, even great. He certainly learned early to be a fierce competitor, seeking some way to outperform his "older, smarter brother." But why did he turn out to be an explorer, a discoverer of secrets hidden in the deep ocean?

The answer seems to be a combination of luck and character. Like many people who have made a name for themselves by visiting new or unknown places or inventing new ways of looking at the world, Ballard has often been in the right place at the right time. He learned to do underwater science in *Alvin* just as a whole new frontier of deep-sea exploration was opening up. He found the wreck of the *Titanic* after others had tried and failed. But he's also stubborn and persistent. He bounces back from failure. At one point in his high school talk, he says, "If you don't quit, you can't fail." It sounds like something his father would have said.

Above all, however, explorers and inventors are people who aren't afraid to challenge conventional wisdom. Often they are laughed at. Sometimes they are persecuted. The history of science is full of stories of men and women who made great discoveries only to be sneered at by their peers and rejected during their own lifetimes. Such people often work by intuition as much as knowledge and reason. Ballard would be the first to admit that luck and guesswork have played a large role in his success. But he would also agree that you won't find anything unless you search for it. Most of all, explorers are curious. They aren't satisfied with the way things are. They always want to see the view from the top of the next hill.

What frontiers will attract the explorers of the future? We have only begun to uncover the mysteries of outer space. And, as Ballard often points out in his lectures, the seventy-one percent of our own planet that is covered with water remains a virtually unknown place. Since 1930, when William Beebe was lowered in a hollow metal globe called a bathysphere attached to a steel cable to the startling depth of 1,426 feet, the modern science of oceanography has grown rapidly. Yet as these words are written, less than one half of one percent of the submerged surface of the earth has been glimpsed by human eyes. In all likelihood it will be robots like *Argo* and *Jason* that perform much of the future exploration of inner space.

Bob Ballard believes that one day soon, just by turning on a television set, you and I will be able to visit these remote places without leaving our own homes. And telepresence will take us not only into the depths of the ocean but to distant planets, long before human beings set foot beyond our solar system.

The next frontiers are as far as your imagination can take you.

# GLOSSARY

**abyssal plain:** The flat area that occupies much of the deep ocean.

*Alvin*: The three-person submarine in which Bob Ballard conducted most of his research and exploration.

**ANGUS:** An acronym for Acoustically NaviGated Underwater Survey, one of the first remotely operated vehicles (ROVs) developed for deep-ocean exploration. It houses still cameras that can take photographs of the seafloor while the vehicle is towed at the end of a long cable.

*Argo*: This remotely operated vehicle (ROV) houses video cameras that shoot footage of the ocean floor.

**Aqua-lung:** The Self-Contained Underwater Breathing Apparatus (SCUBA) that allows divers to breathe underwater.

*Archimède*: The French **bathyscaph** that participated in Project FAMOUS, as well as many other important oceanographic studies.

**ballast tanks:** Tanks on *Alvin* and similar deep submersibles used to control their weight and keep them on an even keel. This is achieved by pumping water (ballast) into or out of the tanks.

**bathyscaph:** A deep **submersible**, able to reach depths of up to ten thousand feet, invented by the Swiss scientist Auguste Piccard. It consists of a small personnel sphere suspended from a large tank of gasoline. The gasoline, which is lighter than water, acts much like the helium that allows a balloon to float in midair or rise and descend.

*Ben Franklin*: A medium-depth submersible, or **mesoscaph**, designed by Jacques Piccard (Auguste's son) that can operate up to a depth of 2,000 feet.

**capstan:** An upright cylinder-shaped device used to raise and lower a ship's anchor or other heavy objects.

**chemosynthesis:** A chemical process by which sulfide-eating bacteria convert hydrogen and carbon dioxide into sugars and starches.

**cold water upwellings:** Areas in the ocean where the prevailing winds blow the surface water away from the coast. This causes the colder, nutrient-rich water below the surface to rise upward. As a result, these areas are feeding grounds for large numbers of fish.

**continental shelf:** The submerged part of a continent that often extends hundreds of miles out from shore.

**davits:** Pairs of small cranes on a ship's side used for launching or hoisting boats. On large ships special davits are set aside for lifeboats.

**debris trail:** The pattern formed by material that falls from a sinking ship.

**fiber-optic cable:** A cable that transmits light along a bundle of thin transparent fibers.

**formaldehyde:** A strong-smelling chemical solution used for preserving biological specimens.

**geochemistry:** The scientific study of the earth's chemistry, the nature of the substances that make up the planet and how these substances change under different conditions.

**geology:** The scientific study of the earth, its origin and its life history as recorded in rocks.

**geophysics:** The scientific study of the physical forces that affect the earth and its environment.

**Gulf Stream:** The ocean current that starts where warm water from the Gulf of Mexico enters the Atlantic Ocean near the Bahamas.

**hydrothermal vents:** Openings in the seafloor through which seawater, heated inside the earth's crust, reenters the ocean.

**JASON Project:** The name for the annual expeditions mounted by the not-for-profit JASON Foundation for Education.

***Jason*:** A remotely operated vehicle (ROV) developed by Bob Ballard for use in deep-ocean exploration. *Jason* is attached to the larger ROV *Argo* by a fiber-optic tether.

***Jason Junior (JJ)*:** The earliest version of *Jason*.

**knot:** The term for one nautical mile (6,076 feet, or about 1.15 miles). Also the common unit used for a ship's speed. One knot equals one nautical mile per hour.

**lava:** Rock that has been heated inside the earth until it becomes a liquid. Also refers to the same rock after it has cooled and hardened.

***Lulu*:** The twin-hulled mother ship originally used by *Alvin*.

**magnetometer:** A device for measuring the strength and direction of a magnetic field.

**marine biology:** The scientific study of the plants and animals that live in fresh or salt water.

**mesoscaph:** A submersible designed to spend long stretches of time at moderate depths of up to two thousand feet.

**oceanography:** The scientific study of the seas and oceans.

**outcrop:** A portion of rock that juts above the sediment-covered ocean floor.

**photosynthesis:** The chemical process by which green plants use the energy from sunlight to convert carbon dioxide and water into sugars and starches.

**plate tectonics:** A scientific theory that says the earth's surface is divided into a number of separate plates. Each of these plates behaves like a huge floating raft but moves so slowly it can't be observed by human beings.

**rift valley:** A steep-sided valley formed when the earth's crust separates and a narrow piece slips downward while the sides bulge upward.

**sea pen:** A feathery looking marine animal closely related to sea anemones and corals.

**seismic survey:** The bouncing of soundwaves off the hard, rocky subbottom beneath the soft sediment layer to draw a clear picture of the ocean subfloor.

**submersible:** Any small pressurized craft that takes human beings beneath the ocean's surface.

**titanium:** A tough, lightweight metal often combined with other metals to make a very strong alloy.

**transponder beacons:** Underwater sound transmitters used in deep-sea navigation.

*Trieste II*: *Trieste* was the first **bathyscaph** designed and built by Auguste Piccard. Later bought by the U. S. Navy, it was fitted with a thicker personnel sphere that permitted it to dive to the deepest part of the ocean. The revamped bathyscaph was renamed *Trieste II*.

**winch:** A drum-shaped device similar to a capstan, used primarily for raising or lowering heavy objects.

# A READING LIST

## FOR YOUNG EXPLORERS

Ballard, Robert D. *Exploring the* Titanic. New York: Scholastic, 1988.

———, with Rick Archbold. *Exploring the* Bismarck. New York: Scholastic, 1991.

———. *The Lost Wreck of the* Isis. New York: Scholastic, 1990.

Beebe, Charles W. *Half Mile Down.* New York: Duell, Sloan and Pearce, 1962.

Berger, Melvin. *Oceanography Lab.* New York: John Day, 1973.

Blair, Carvel H. *Exploring the Sea: Oceanography Today.* New York: Random House, 1986.

Burgess, Robert F. *Ships Beneath the Sea: A History of Subs and Submersibles.* New York: McGraw-Hill, 1975.

Cook, Jan Leslie. *The Mysterious Undersea World.* Washington, D.C.: National Geographic Society, 1980.

Cousteau, Jacques-Yves, with Fred Dumas. *The Silent World.* New York: Harper & Row, 1953.

Earle, Sylvia, Giddings, Al, and the editors of the National Geographic Society. *Exploring the Deep Frontier: The Adventures of Man in the Sea.* Washington, D.C.: National Geographic Society, 1980.

Grant, Neil. *The Great Atlas of Discovery.* New York: Knopf, 1992.

Greene, Carol. *Jacques Cousteau: Man of the Oceans.* Chicago: Childrens Press, 1990.

Groves, Don. *The Oceans: A Book of Questions and Answers.* New York: John Wiley, 1989.

Kaharl, Victoria. *Water Baby: The Story of* Alvin. New York: Oxford University Press, 1990.

Piccard, Jacques. *Seven Miles Down: The Story of the Bathyscaph* Trieste. New York: Putnam, 1961.

Polking, Kirk. *Oceans of the World: Our Essential Resource.* New York: Philomel Books, 1983.

Shenton, Edward H. *Diving for Science: The Story of the Deep Submersible.* New York: W. W. Norton, 1972.

Verne, Jules. *Twenty Thousand Leagues Under the Sea.* New York: Scholastic, 1992.

# ACKNOWLEDGMENTS

BOB BALLARD MAY NOT AGREE WITH EVERYTHING I'VE written about him in this book, but he graciously cooperated in every way to make its writing a pleasure, and the result as accurate as possible. His mother, Harriett Ballard, and his brother, Richard Ballard, also willingly shared their memories and insights, especially about Bob's childhood. In addition, several people who knew Bob as a young man helped fill in important gaps: Robert Norris, Kenneth Norris, and Karen Pryor. And I'd especially like to thank Bob Ballard's assistant, Linda Lucier, who answered every request for help with cheerfulness and alacrity.

The following individuals and institutions provided essential information for the text: Archie Graham; McDonald's Corporation; Carolyn Rainey, Scripps Institution of Oceanography Archives; Leslie Dance, Sea Life Park; Shelly Lauzon, Woods Hole Oceanographic Institution; Susan Lewis and Rebecca Squires of The JASON Project.

As usual, the team at Madison Press gave me enthusiastic and highly skilled support, but I'd like to particularly mention two of them. Sara Borins ruthlessly tracked down stray facts. And my editor, Mireille Majoor, made many astute suggestions and skillfully brought my often errant prose into line. And finally, thanks to Amy Scheinberg at Scholastic for her perceptive comments on the original draft.

RICK ARCHBOLD
TORONTO, JUNE 1993

# INDEX

142

PICTURE CREDITS

**Front Cover:** George F. Mobley © National Geographic Society. **Back flap:** Peter Buckley. **Page 15:** *(All)* Courtesy Mrs. Harriett Ballard. **Page 29 :** *(All)* Courtesy Mrs. Harriett Ballard. **Page 39:** *(Top)* Robert D. Ballard *(Bottom)* Courtesy Mrs. Harriet Ballard. **Page 57:** *(Top)* Robert D. Ballard © Odyssey Corporation *(Bottom)* Jack McMaster/Margo Stahl. **Page 65:** *(Top)* Emory Kristof © National Geographic Society *(Bottom)* WHOI. **Page 69:** *(Top)* WHOI *(Bottom)* Emory Kristof © National Geographic Society. **Page 79:** *(Top)* WHOI *(Bottom)* WHOI, photograph by Carl Wirsen. **Page 83:** *(Top)* WHOI, photograph by John Donnell *(Bottom)* WHOI. **Page 87:** *(Top)* Ulster Folk and Transport Museum *(Bottom)* The Shipbuilder. **Page 91:** *(Top)* Painting by Ken Marschall *(Bottom)* National Archives. **Page 99:** *(All)* WHOI. **Page 107:** *(All)* Emory Kristof © National Geographic Society. **Page 112:** *(Top)* Painting by Ken Marschall *(Bottom left)* WHOI *(Bottom right)* Robert D. Ballard © Odyssey. **Page 113:** *(Top)* Painting by Ken Marschall *(Bottom left and right)* WHOI. **Page 117:** *(Top)* Painting by Ken Marschall *(Top and bottom right)* WHOI. **Page 125:** *(Top)* Painting by Ken Marschall *(Bottom)* Quest Group. **Page 129:** *(Top)* Joseph M. Bailey © National Geographic Society *(Bottom)* Painting by Ken Marschall.

# *Titanic:* Destination Disaster

BY JOHN L. LIPP

PAPERBACK **PLUS**

## CHARACTERS

| | |
|---|---|
| FIRST OFFICER MURDOCK | MARY SLOAN |
| QUARTERMASTER HITCHENS | EDITH RUSSELL |
| FLEET, THE LOOKOUT | JOHN JACOB ASTOR |
| LAWRENCE BEESLEY | MRS. JOHN JACOB ASTOR |
| CAPTAIN SMITH | ISADOR STRAUS |
| THREE PASSENGERS | MRS. ISADOR STRAUS |
| THOMAS ANDREWS | BENJAMIN GUGGENHEIM |
| OFFICER WILDE | FIRST OFFICER LIGHTOLLER |
| OFFICER BOXHALL | ETCHES, THE STEWARD |

## AUTHOR'S NOTE

When the *Titanic* first set sail, it was considered the most luxurious, fastest, and, at 46,000 tons, the largest ship afloat. Among its many features were a Turkish bath, swimming pool, squash court, and a grand stairway that stood over six stories high from its base to the top of the domed glass skylight that covered it. Its hull was divided into sixteen watertight compartments designed to stay afloat even if any two of those compartments were flooded. Because of this special design, the *Titanic* was thought to be unsinkable.

**TIME:** Sunday, April 14, and Monday, April 15, 1912.

**SETTING:** Split stage: at left, the engine room, and at right, boat deck of the *Titanic*. Chair left represents lookout's tower at front of ship.

**AT RISE:** Stage is dimly lit. Spotlight comes up left.

FLEET, *the lookout, is staring intently off left.* FIRST OFFICER MURDOCK *and* QUARTERMASTER HITCHENS *stand behind him, in engine room.*

**FLEET** (*Yelling*):  Iceberg, dead ahead!

**MURDOCK** (*Urgently*):  Turn the wheel starboard, Hitchens. (HITCHENS *motions as if turning wheel.*)

**HITCHENS:**  Aye, aye, sir.

**MURDOCK:**  Now, full speed ahead. (HITCHENS *motions as if pulling throttle.*)

**HITCHENS:**  Aye, sir . . . What next?

**MURDOCK:**  We've done all that is humanly possible, Hitchens. All we can do now is wait. (MURDOCK *and* HITCHENS *continue to look off left.* BEESLEY *enters, crosses center, and addresses audience.*)

**BEESLEY:**  And thirty-seven seconds later, we hit. (BEESLEY, FLEET, HITCHENS, *and* MURDOCK *jolt slightly to left, as if feeling impact of being hit.* CAPTAIN SMITH *enters hurriedly and crosses left.*)

**CAPTAIN SMITH** (*Tensely*):  Mr. Murdock, what happened?

**MURDOCK** (*Pointing, panicky*):  An iceberg, sir. We did all we could, but she was too close.

**SMITH:**  Close the emergency doors!

**MURDOCK:**  Done, sir.

**BEESLEY:**  But by then it was already too late. (*Spotlight goes out left, comes up on* TWO PASSENGERS, *who enter right.*)

**1ST PASSENGER** (*Panicky*): What was that?

**2ND PASSENGER:** I think we hit something.

**1ST PASSENGER** (*Puzzled*): But what? It was only a slight jolt.

**2ND PASSENGER:** Perhaps some debris from another ship?

**1ST PASSENGER:** Well, whatever it was, it can't be anything too serious.

**2ND PASSENGER:** I'm sure it's nothing to worry about. After all, this is the world's most luxurious ocean line! (*They ad lib quiet conversation as* BEESLEY *speaks.*)

**BEESLEY:** Welcome to the *Titanic*. She is not only the world's most luxurious ocean liner, but at ninety-two feet wide, 882 feet long, and eleven stories high, she is the world's largest. (PASSENGERS, MURDOCK, HITCHENS, SMITH, *and* FLEET *turn to the audience.*)

**ALL:** Unsinkable!

**BEESLEY:** Or so we thought. (FLEET, HITCHENS, MURDOCK, *and* SMITH *exit.*) But on the *Titanic*'s maiden voyage of April 14, 1912, she hit an iceberg and sank two and a half miles to the bottom of the Atlantic Ocean, taking with her 1,522 men, women, and children.

**LAWRENCE BEESLEY**

**1ST PASSENGER:** Including me. (*Exits*)

**2ND PASSENGER:** And me. (*Exits*)

**BEESLEY:** I was one of the lucky ones. One of only 700 people who survived that night. Why me? I've often wondered that. Perhaps it's as simple a fact as that I was in the right place at the right time, as much as the *Titanic* was in the wrong place. My name is Lawrence Beesley, and I am a schoolteacher making my first trip to America as a second-class passenger. (*After a pause*) I'll never forget that night on the *Titanic*. The sea was dead calm, barely a ripple. And the air was ice-cold. Without a moon to shed light, the ship was surrounded by darkness. But the sky was so incredibly clear. Each star that night was exceptionally bright. It was almost as if they were alive, talking to each other, and all the while watching helplessly the catastrophe that was unfolding on the earth below. (BEESLEY *moves upstage, passing* THOMAS ANDREWS *as he enters.* ANDREWS *and* SMITH *move center.* BEESLEY *turns, back to audience.*) That's Mr. Thomas Andrews (ANDREWS *nods.*), the managing director of White Star Lines, the company that designed and built the *Titanic*. It was said that Mr. Andrews knew every rivet, every nail, every piece of steel, and every piece of fabric that went into the creation of the *Titanic*. He is talking with Edward J. Smith, the Captain of the *Titanic*, who had planned to retire after taking the *Titanic* on her maiden voyage. Of all the people who died that night, I don't think any two were quite as tragic as Mr. Andrews and Captain Smith. It is now 12:00 a.m., twenty minutes after the *Titanic* hit the iceberg. (BEESLEY *exits.*)

**SMITH:** Mr. Andrews, you know this ship like the back of your hand. What is your assessment, sir?

**ANDREWS:** Captain Smith, after inspecting the damage, I'd say we have maybe one, one and a half hours left. When we hit the iceberg on the right-hand side, it created an opening that has filled the first four water-tight compartments with water. The water has slowly overflowed from one compartment to the next. As each compartment fills, she is slowly tipping forward, allowing the weight of the water to bring her down. Within an hour, I estimate her entire bow will be under water.

**SMITH** (*Gravely*): If only I had heeded the ice warnings that came in earlier. Perhaps . . .

**ANDREWS:** Captain Smith, we've no time to think about what should have been done. As each moment passes, the speed that she's sinking will increase until . . . (ANDREWS *stops, shakes head.*)

**SMITH** (*Yelling urgently*): Officer Wilde! Officer Boxhall! (OFFICERS WILDE *and* BOXHALL *rush on, across to* CAPTAIN.)

**WILDE:** Yes, sir.

**SMITH:** Officer Wilde, uncover the lifeboats. We will begin evacuating the *Titanic* in an orderly and controlled fashion. There are to be no rumors, no panic. Is that understood?

**WILDE:** Yes sir. (WILDE *exits.*)

**SMITH:** Officer Boxhall, wake up Second Officer Lightoller, Third Officer Pitman, and Fifth Officer Lowe. I will need each of you to assist with the orderly evacuation of the passengers.

**BOXHALL:** Sir?

**SMITH:** Yes, Officer Boxhall?

**BOXHALL:** We have only enough lifeboats to accommodate 1,178 of the passengers, sir.

**SMITH:** Yes, Officer Boxhall?

**BOXHALL:** But we have over 2,200 passengers on board, sir.

**SMITH** (*Grimly*): Women and children first, Mr. Boxhall. Women and children first.

**BOXHALL:** Yes, sir. (BOXHALL *exits*.)

**ANDREWS:** Incredible isn't it, Captain Smith. There are only enough lifeboats to accommodate half our passengers, yet we have more than the British Board of Trade ever required.

THOMAS ANDREWS

**SMITH:** Perhaps future generations will learn from our errors, Mr. Andrews. . . . If you'll excuse me, I need to have the wireless room send out distress calls. At this time our only hope is for another ship in the vicinity to rescue the remaining passengers before we disappear forever. (SMITH *exits.*)

**ANDREWS:** Disappear . . . forever. (ANDREWS *exits, passing* BEESLEY, *who enters, stands upstage.*)

**BEESLEY:** It was at that moment that Mr. Andrews realized the *Titanic*, his monument to the twentieth century and the power of technology, was as fragile as the men who had built her, as fragile as the people who would disappear with her . . . forever. (MARY SLOAN *enters with* 3RD PASSENGER. *They cross center.*)

**SLOAN:** Now, don't worry, it couldn't be that bad. (SLOAN *and* 3RD PASSENGER *ad lib quiet conversation as* BEESLEY *speaks.*)

**BEESLEY:** That is Mary Sloan, a stewardess on the *Titanic*, and one of its many heroes that night.

**3RD PASSENGER** (*Nervously*): But, Miss Sloan, why have we stopped?

**SLOAN:** Well, whatever hit us probably did some minor damage to the ship. And knowing how proud the captain is of the *Titanic*, he probably doesn't want to continue on until he's sure that she is in tip-top shape.

**3RD PASSENGER:** But what if there's leakage?

**SLOAN:** The pumps will handle it. (*In comforting tone*) Now, don't worry. (3RD PASSENGER *exits, passing* ANDREWS, *who enters.*) Mr. Andrews?

**ANDREWS:** Yes, Miss Sloan?

**SLOAN:** Is everything all right, sir?

**ANDREWS:** I'm afraid not, Miss Sloan. I think it would be wise to have everyone put their life jackets on over warm clothing and have them assemble on the boat deck. But, please, I don't want panic. It's imperative that we handle this with complete dignity. After all, we are British.

**SLOAN:** Yes, sir.

**ANDREWS:** (*Calling after her as she begins to exit*): Oh, and Miss Sloan? When I say everyone must put on their life jackets, I mean you as well. (SLOAN *looks at him meaningfully, then exits.* ANDREWS *watches her exit, then after a moment, follows her out.*)

**BEESLEY** (*Crossing center*): Mary Sloan would stay on the ship until 1:45 in the morning, helping passengers into the lifeboats. If Mr. Andrews had not seen her, she would have stayed and gone down with the ship. He ordered her onto the last lifeboat to leave the *Titanic,* number four. All that remained were collapsible boats, actually large rafts. Not nearly enough for the fifteen hundred people who remained. Ironically, when lifeboat number four was lowered, twenty places in the boat were left empty. Why? (EDITH RUSSELL *enters, crosses to stand next to* BEESLEY.)

**RUSSELL:** I don't think we'll ever know why. But it wasn't just lifeboat four. Lifeboat number seven, the first lifeboat to be lowered into the cold Atlantic approximately one hour after the *Titanic* first hit the iceberg, had only twenty-eight people aboard.

**BEESLEY:** It was made to carry sixty-five.

**RUSSELL:** And it happened over and over again on that terrible night.

**BEESLEY:** This is Miss Edith Russell, a fashion correspondent for the magazine, *Women's Wear*.

**RUSSELL:** The *Titanic* was the most fantastic ocean liner I had ever seen. Yet, from the minute I stepped aboard, I felt it was almost too fantastic. It seemed as if man had perhaps gone too far this time. As beautiful as the *Titanic* was, I couldn't help but feel that something terrible was going to happen. How I wish I had been wrong! (*As* RUSSELL *exits, she passes* MR. *and* MRS. JOHN JACOB ASTOR, MR. *and* MRS. ISADOR STRAUS, *and* BENJAMIN GUGGENHEIM.)

**BEESLEY:** Among those who were aboard the *Titanic* that night were some of the wealthiest people alive. One in particular could have bought the *Titanic* several times over. His name was John Jacob Astor, and he was among the richest men in the world. (JOHN JACOB ASTOR *and* MRS. ASTOR *move center.*)

**MRS. ASTOR:** They say we should put these life jackets on. I don't understand, darling. How could such a simple device keep one afloat in the ocean?

**ASTOR:** No need to worry. Why, you'll be quite dry and very much afloat in a lifeboat, my dear.

**MRS. ASTOR:** You'll come with me, won't you?

**ASTOR:** I'm afraid not. The officers have informed me that only women and children will be allowed in the lifeboats tonight. I'm sure it's just a precaution, but after all, I wouldn't be much of a gentleman if I refused their orders, would I?

**BEESLEY:** And so Mrs. Astor entered lifeboat number four.

**ASTOR** (*As* MRS. ASTOR *exits*): Don't worry, my dear. I'll get another boat and follow just behind you. I promise.

**BEESLEY:** But by then it was too late. Of the men that were allowed on a lifeboat, most were crew members who were placed on the boats as oarsmen. John Jacob Astor would never see his wife again. (ASTOR *exits.* MR. *and* MRS. ISADOR STRAUS *move center as* FIRST OFFICER LIGHTOLLER *enters.*)

**LIGHTOLLER:** Mrs. Straus, please, you must come with me.

**MRS. STRAUS:** And leave my husband? Never!

**BEESLEY:** Mr. and Mrs. Isador Straus, the owners of Macy's department stores. They had been married for over forty years.

**STRAUS:** Please, my dear. You must take your place in one of the lifeboats. It's your only chance.

**MRS. STRAUS:** I have spent my life with you, Isador. Where you go, I go. (LIGHTOLLER, *upset, exits.* MR. *and* MRS. STRAUS, *arm and arm, immediately follow him out.*)

**BEESLEY:** The last anyone ever saw of Mr. and Mrs. Straus, they were on the promenade deck, sitting side by side in deck chairs, peacefully waiting for the end. (BENJAMIN GUGGENHEIM *moves center.*)

**GUGGENHEIM:** Steward Etches? (STEWARD ETCHES *enters.*)

**ETCHES:** Yes, Mr. Guggenheim?

**BEESLEY:** Mr. Benjamin Guggenheim, an industrial giant who was traveling without his wife on this journey. Like all first-class passengers, he was rarely without a private steward at his side.

MR. & MRS.
ISADOR STRAUS

157

**GUGGENHEIM:** I shall require your assistance changing into my evening clothes.

**ETCHES** (*Surprised*): Sir?

**GUGGENHEIM:** Etches, you've taken good care of me on this journey. I have only one more request for you.

**ETCHES:** Anything, sir.

**GUGGENHEIM:** If you should survive, please locate my wife and tell her that I have done my duty and have gone down like a gentleman. (GUGGENHEIM *and* ETCHES *exit.*)

**BEESLEY:** Etches did indeed survive, and relayed to Mr. Guggenheim's family just how distinguished he looked in his full dress evening clothes. (EDITH RUSSELL *enters.*)

**RUSSELL:** It was now 2:17 a.m., and those of us who had found a place in a lifeboat watched in horror as the *Titanic*'s brief but magnificent life came to an end.

**BEESLEY:** First, Captain Smith released from duty the remaining crew members who had so bravely done their duty until the very end. (SMITH *enters.*)

**SMITH:** Gentlemen, you have done all that is humanly possible. You are hereby released from duty. It is now every man for himself. (SMITH *exits.*)

**RUSSELL:** And then he was gone. As sea captains had done for generations before him, Captain Smith prepared to go down with his ship.

**BEESLEY:** At 2:18 a.m., the ship's bow was completely underwater, and the stern was lifted up in the air. There was a tremendous crash as everything that wasn't bolted down came careening forward. And then she broke in half, the bow crashing 12,460 feet to the bottom of the ocean.

**RUSSELL:** The stern then slowly righted itself, almost as if it were going to resist the forces of nature and float forever. But soon it, too, filled with water and began to tilt forward.

**BEESLEY:** And at 2:20 a.m., it disappeared completely. The *Titanic* was gone, and for a brief moment there was only silence.

**RUSSELL:** Where the *Titanic* once was, the water was now filled with hundreds of people, clinging to whatever piece of wreckage they could find. One clung to a boat chair, another to a piece of wood.

**BEESLEY:** But the water was freezing cold that night, and most people lasted for only a short time before the cold and shock overtook them. One by one they became victims of the frigid north Atlantic Ocean.

**RUSSELL:** The lifeboats floated in the water for nearly two hours before another ship, the *Carpathia*, came to our rescue. One by one the lifeboats were unloaded until finally the Captain of the *Carpathia* was convinced that all the survivors were on board.

**BEESLEY:** At 8:50 the following morning, the *Carpathia* headed to New York, carrying 705 survivors from the great unsinkable ship, the *Titanic*.

**RUSSELL:** One thousand, five hundred and twenty-two people died that night. Men, women, and children.

**BEESLEY:** The majority of those who died were third-class passengers. Many were not allowed onto the upper decks until it was too late. By the time they did manage to reach the deck, all the lifeboats were gone.

**RUSSELL:** Most were immigrants who were coming to America in search of a better life.

**BEESLEY:** It was a dream that never came true.

**RUSSELL:** They say that some good comes from all tragedies, and the *Titanic* was no exception.

**BEESLEY:** An International Conference for the Safety of Life at Sea was held in London in 1913. From that conference came several measures meant to ensure that a tragedy like the *Titanic* would never happen again. (FLEET, FIRST OFFICER MURDOCK, QUARTERMASTER HITCHENS, THREE PASSENGERS, THOMAS ANDREWS, CAPTAIN SMITH, OFFICER WILDE, OFFICER BOXHALL, MARY SLOAN, MR. *and* MRS. ASTOR, MR. *and* MRS. STRAUS, FIRST OFFICER LIGHTOLLER, BENJAMIN GUGGENHEIM, *and* STEWARD ETCHES *reenter.*)

**1ST PASSENGER:** From then on, all ocean-going ships were required to have enough lifeboats to accommodate all passengers and crew.

**2ND PASSENGER:** All ships were to be outfitted with wireless sets.

**FLEET:** The firing of rockets or distress calls was to be done only for actual emergencies.

**SMITH:** Captains would never again ignore ice warnings. They would slow down and, if necessary, change their course.

**WILDE:** An International Ice Patrol was created.

**BOXHALL:** Eventually this international patrol became part of the United States Coast Guard.

**ANDREWS:** In memory of the *Titanic* and those who were lost at sea, every year the Coast Guard drops a wreath on the site where the *Titanic* was last seen before going down.

**SLOAN:** But what happened to the *Titanic* after she disappeared below the ocean's surface on that cold night?

**3RD PASSENGER:** We knew approximately where she was, 350 miles southeast of Newfoundland.

**ASTOR:** Two miles below the surface.

**MRS. ASTOR:** But nobody knew the exact spot of her grave.

**STRAUS:** For years people talked of finding the *Titanic* and of the great treasures that went down with her.

**MRS. STRAUS:** But it wasn't until 1985 that a combination of technology and determination made such a dream a reality.

**LIGHTOLLER:** On September 1, 1985, Dr. Robert Ballard and his team of scientists found the wreck of the *Titanic*.

**GUGGENHEIM:** Using a submarine and a small robot with an attached camera, they went two and a half miles to the bottom of the ocean and once again human eyes were able to see the *Titanic*.

**ETCHES:** Only this time it was a much different ship.

**MURDOCK:** Lying in two sections, her hull was in remarkably good shape.

**HITCHENS:** The carved wood that once graced her interior had long since rotted away, yet her huge metal frame was still very much intact.

**BEESLEY:** But her stern was now nothing more than a twisted piece of wreckage.

**RUSSELL:** In between the two sections was a debris field of artifacts from the *Titanic*. Not just pieces from the ship, but mementos of the passengers. Each item was a memory of a human being.

**SLOAN:** A tea cup.

**MRS. ASTOR:** Silver serving dishes.

**MRS. STRAUS:** Wine bottles still corked.

**ANDREWS:** Bathtubs.

**3RD PASSENGER:** Deck chairs.

**1ST PASSENGER:** Hair brushes.

**SMITH:** And saddest of all, lying next to each other, were three pairs of shoes.

**BEESLEY:** Sometimes, as the years march on, I think back to that voyage and to the wonderful times we had before that awful moment when the *Titanic* hit the iceberg. I can still see people laughing, dancing, and celebrating the maiden voyage of the grandest ocean liner the world had ever known—the *Titanic*!

**ALL** (*Raising hands in tribute*): Unsinkable! (*All freeze as* SMITH *walks forward, looking at each actor. One by one, they exit, obviously sad, heads down. When* SMITH *is alone, he speaks his last line.*)

**SMITH:** Or so we thought. (*He exits as curtain falls.*)

**THE END**

# Exploring the
## *Titanic*

This scale drawing
shows the enormous
distance between the
*Knorr* on the surface
and the *Titanic* wreck
on the ocean floor.

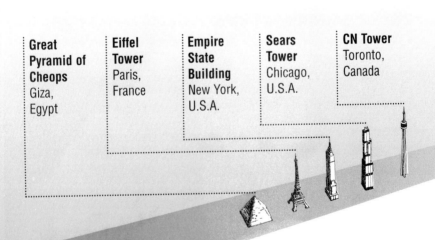

| Great Pyramid of Cheops Giza, Egypt | Eiffel Tower Paris, France | Empire State Building New York, U.S.A. | Sears Tower Chicago, U.S.A. | CN Tower Toronto, Canada |

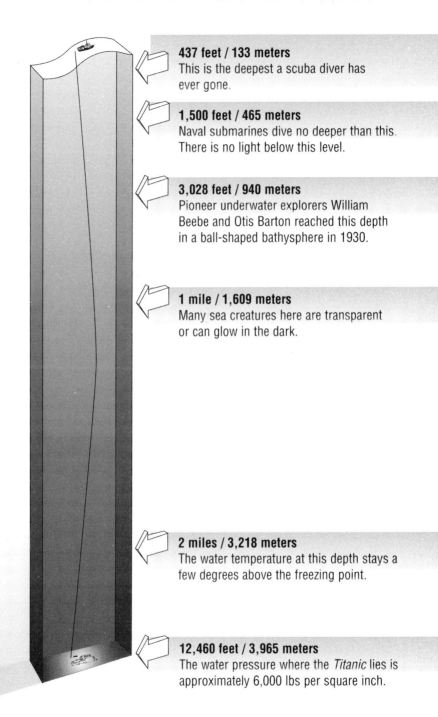

### 437 feet / 133 meters
This is the deepest a scuba diver has ever gone.

### 1,500 feet / 465 meters
Naval submarines dive no deeper than this. There is no light below this level.

### 3,028 feet / 940 meters
Pioneer underwater explorers William Beebe and Otis Barton reached this depth in a ball-shaped bathysphere in 1930.

### 1 mile / 1,609 meters
Many sea creatures here are transparent or can glow in the dark.

### 2 miles / 3,218 meters
The water temperature at this depth stays a few degrees above the freezing point.

### 12,460 feet / 3,965 meters
The water pressure where the *Titanic* lies is approximately 6,000 lbs per square inch.